W9-CSM-555

EMPOWERED
GARDENS

Architects and Designers at Home

Carol Soucek King, Ph.D.

Foreword by **Michael Graves,** FAIA

PBC INTERNATIONAL, INC.

Distributor to the book trade in the United States and Canada
Rizzoli International Publications
through St. Martin's Press
175 Fifth Avenue
New York, NY 10010

Distributor to the art trade in the United States and Canada
PBC International, Inc.
One School Street
Glen Cove, NY 11542

Distributor throughout the rest of the world
Hearst Books International
1350 Avenue of the Americas
New York, NY 10019

Copyright © 1997 by
PBC International, Inc.
All rights reserved. No part of this book may be
reproduced in any form whatsoever without
written permission of the copyright owner,
PBC International, Inc.
One School Street, Glen Cove, NY 11542

Library of Congress Cataloging–in–Publication Data

Empowered gardens : architects & designers at home / [compiled by]
    Carol Soucek King.
            p.   cm.
    Includes index.
    ISBN 0-86636-433-1 (hb : alk. paper). — ISBN 0-86636-422-6 (pbk. : alk. paper)
    1. Gardens. 2. Landscape architects—Homes and haunts. 3. Architects—
Homes and haunts. 4. Interior decorators—Homes and haunts. 5. Gardens—
Pictorial works. 6. Landscape architects—Homes and haunts—Pictorial
works. 7. Architects—Homes and haunts—Pictorial works. 8. Interior
decorators—Homes and haunts—Pictorial works.   I. King, Carol Soucek.
SB465.E54 1997
712'.6—dc20   97-11168
                                                        CIP

CAVEAT– Information in this text is believed accurate, and will pose no
problem for the student or casual reader. However, the author was often
constrained by information contained in signed release forms, information
that could have been in error or not included at all. Any misinformation
(or lack of information) is the result of failure in these attestations. The
author has done whatever is possible to insure accuracy.

Designed by Garrett Schuh

Color separation, printing and binding by
Dai Nippon Group, Hong Kong

10 9 8 7 6 5 4 3 2 1

Printed in Hong Kong

To those who feel empowered by
the spirit of The Earth and who long
to sing its songs!

CONTENTS

FOREWORD

Michael Graves, FAIA,
Architect

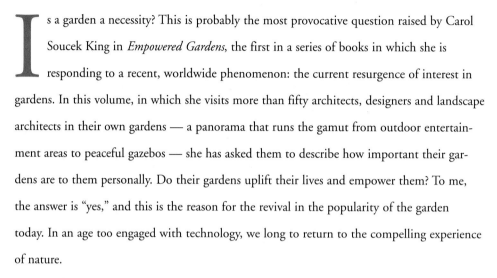

I s a garden a necessity? This is probably the most provocative question raised by Carol Soucek King in *Empowered Gardens*, the first in a series of books in which she is responding to a recent, worldwide phenomenon: the current resurgence of interest in gardens. In this volume, in which she visits more than fifty architects, designers and landscape architects in their own gardens — a panorama that runs the gamut from outdoor entertainment areas to peaceful gazebos — she has asked them to describe how important their gardens are to them personally. Do their gardens uplift their lives and empower them? To me, the answer is "yes," and this is the reason for the revival in the popularity of the garden today. In an age too engaged with technology, we long to return to the compelling experience of nature.

Of course, one can say that there is a different level of importance between a building, which is a necessity in terms of shelter, and architecture and landscape architecture. The latter are cultural inventions, as are literature, poetry and music, and some may not consider these to be necessities at all. Yet, for myself and for the others whose work is reflected in the following pages, understanding where one is — in the landscape looking at a house or in the house looking at the garden — is every bit as important as the roof overhead.

The garden is a place of transition. It is that space between places that sometimes needs definition and sometimes does not. The garden takes that which is ambiguous and gives it value.

The garden is a way of life. There's a kind of social engagement between people and the landscape. Wandering out-of-doors, taking in the sounds, smells and visual aspects of nature, affects one's attitude. You are not the same person as when you are indoors.

Finally, for most people, one's own garden is primarily about domesticity. Anyone can make a place outside with which to have a relationship, and once you do, once you have recognized those aspects of something completely natural that are important to you, then it becomes your garden and everything that happens to it and in it becomes important to you. And one doesn't have to be a landscape architect to gain from watering and feeding one's

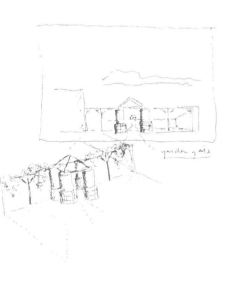

plants and watching them grow. The responsibility of tending one's garden helps one's humanity. Whether one's garden is traditional or innovative, whether it's a formal French garden or a more natural English one, an expansive landscape or a simple roof garden, three aspects of one's own garden remain supreme: the first is looking at it; the second is tending it; and the third is using it. The true spirit of the garden springs from the joy of living outside as well as inside.

I was in Tuscany a couple of years ago and was invited to lunch at a simple farm-style house that was charming but not grand in any way. The garden was not pretentious at all, just fine pea gravel, no grass. Under a span of trees there was a long farm table covered with a crude piece of rose-patterned oilcloth and surrounded by simple, unmatched wooden chairs with rush seats. The table was laden with cheese, olives and a few carafes of wine. We were served a little salad, then pasta, still later some simple fruit and coffee. And all that took two-and-a-half to three hours — for we had all sat and talked and talked and talked! In this delightful outdoor setting we were able to focus on conversation and getting to know each other. Amid a feeling of uninterrupted conviviality that seems all too rare today for many of us (though it seemed as if our hosts did this every day of the year), life seemed richer, brighter, deeper.

On leaving that house and our Italian hosts, I thought how happy I was to have been there. I also began to reflect on how my own life was slightly impoverished because it didn't have enough of that kind of simplicity, the kind of simplicity that can only be found in nature, a simplicity that can combat other less meaningful, acquired tastes as well as the technology that seems sometimes to choke our deeper sense of humanity.

I remember that day and now try to repeat it as often as I can in my own garden. The experience seemed a kind of paradigm for my own life. I learned something about how fulfilling such a moment in the garden can be to me. And I hope that through the compelling array presented in *Empowered Gardens* others will find similar inspiration.

PREFACE

Carol Soucek King, Ph.D.

A mid a world increasingly caught up in a perplexing morass of technology, there has developed an immense desire for age-old processes at one with The Earth — for protecting, nurturing and being a part of Nature. The result has been a revolutionary growth of interest in the garden. Indeed, when my husband and I developed our own property, I found that my interest in gardening had become a passion.

Empowered Gardens explores this revolution through renowned architects, designers and landscape specialists who share their thoughts regarding their own private gardens. How do the ways they have landscaped the property around their own homes reflect or differ from the style and feeling of the projects they create for others? What kinds of plant and hardscape materials have they used and why? How do they incorporate their gardens into their daily lives? Do they just relax in them, or do they actually toil in them? What to them is the most important aspect of this, their personal piece of Earth?

Through sharing their poolscapes, desertscapes, seaside gazebos and urban patios located in the Americas, Europe, the Far East and Southeast Asia, these designers offer a myriad of inventive ideas for making the most of one's own garden, whether large or small. And, as each of them explains, the carefully planned and lovingly tended garden offers the same opportunity that it holds for his or her clients — physical, psychological and spiritual enrichment.

Certainly in our own garden, my husband and I have found endlessly abundant rejuvenation and joy.

EXPLORERS

Garden as Cloister

"Similar to the cloister in a monastery, my garden in Dallas is totally enclosed to offer seclusion from the elements of the city which surrounds it.

"Since the early 1980s I have been constructing this garden from 'found' objects, architectural remnants, pieces of broken tile .... The unusual result offers a large dose of the element of surprise I try to incorporate in all my projects, although those done for clients tend to be more conservative. The style of my house, which is located on a 100-by-120-foot lot, is funky English with an Italian accent — and that's also an apt description

for the garden connecting the loggia to my tile studio.

"I use my garden morning through night. The recent addition of an outdoor shower allows me to incorporate the garden's natural, sensual ambience into my daily bathing routine. Most evenings, even chilly ones when I light a glowing blaze in the outdoor fireplace, the garden serves as outdoor rooms for entertaining. And, sunup to sundown, I use the garden for inspiration, the open sky for clearing my thoughts."

above *The loggia, built from discarded antiques and stone, provides an old-world Italianate dining area all year long.*

opposite *A tapestry of tile mosaic joins an equally colorful canary, while half columns create windows to see into and out of the seating area.*

Photography by Barry Lewis

Robert Bellamy Landscape Designer

Dallas, *Texas*

above *A table inlaid with tile mosaic adds a note of enchantment to an intimate dining area near the outdoor fireplace.*

left *The aromatic shrub, Powis Castle artemisia, highlights the organic nature of found stone, which is juxtaposed with architectonic elements elsewhere.*

left *A fence made from sculptor Stuart Kraft's iron cut-outs stands on a base of organic rock, making a dramatic backdrop for this boxwood and rosebush topiary. Flanking the view are two Italian cypress trees.*

left *"Birds are a lovely addition to a soulful space": Robert Bellamy framed by a skewed "birdhouse" made from a weathered wooden fence.*

below *Stone columns with natural rough-cedar beams create a monumental arbor for three varieties of rose — New Dawn, Sombreuil and Zephirine Drouhin.*

right *A stone column draped with a garland of roses frames the romantic view of a wisteria-covered tree. Its shade envelops the fountain, each a welcome relief during hot Texas summers.*

Color! Texture!

"With sixteen acres at LongHouse, my home on Long Island, I have the opportunity for several expressions: A woodsy arboretum while existing oaks and hickories are being replaced by choice specimens … large lawns for sculpture and performing arts events … sunken formal gardens … dozens of informal borders … gardens by color … and demonstration gardens for special collections such as the two hundred daffodil cultivars, one hundred types of ornamental grasses and fifty of bamboo.

"I feel a great similarity between working with the texture, color and structure of plant materials and working with the same qualities in yarns/textiles. The scale, of course, is different. And both fabrics and furniture stay put, while plant material changes.

"I am in the garden more hours than in the house and dine there when possible. When not, we dine in one of the rooms overlooking the garden. I frown on guests who lurk indoors during daylight. The garden is also my therapy. As almost all weather is good for some garden activity, we transplant in the rain and do heavy pruning after snowfall.

"This weekend gardening is the backbone of my schedule. Because I must travel, I measure time by 'weekends away' — there are not many, as I fly in Fridays from all over the world."

above *Looking north beyond Peter's Pond is South Gate of LongHouse, modeled on Ise Temple, the seventh-century Shinto shrine.*

right *Rectangular beds, set in potato-size gravel that drains water to the pond, are planted with perovskia, gaura and small mallows.*

Photography above by Elliott Kaufman Other photography courtesy of Jack Lenor Larsen

Jack Lenor Larsen Textile Designer

right *Looking east from the quarry-tiled dancing plaza in front of the pond. The black Ming pots were acquired by Jack Lenor Larsen while traveling in India.*

below *"This weekend gardening is the backbone of my life schedule": Rarely seen without gloves and garden tools, Jack Lenor Larsen at the edge of Peter's Pond.*

right *Beyond the dancing plaza, steps at left lead up to the moon bridge and into the conservatory. To the right are some of the twelve rectangular beds of perennials set into a gravel drainage pad. The seemingly accidental placement of Grace Kowlton's masonry spheres throughout the great lawn suggests an otherworldly feeling.*

Under the Bridges

"It was under the bridges spanning the Arroyo Seco in Pasadena, California, that my husband Richard King and I found the property where we would build our home in the late 1970s. We both knew what we wanted ... a sense of being hidden away in nature ... a place more rustic and wild than refined and manicured ... and a garden easy to maintain.

"Architects Conrad Buff III and Donald C. Hensman helped us find the property, the last available land located so closely to the 134 Freeway Bridge and the historic Colorado Street Bridge. All other land in sight is a public park, complete with a creek that forms our meandering eastern border. This, to us, provided the ideal setting for whatever we would develop, and that turned out to be the main house and swimming pool, the guest house and tennis court six years later, and then, almost eight years after that, the gazebo.

"To connect the three structures, Conrad and Don, with Howard and Tom Oshiyama, artfully rearranged river rock and boulders found on the property. The result is a groomed effect surrounding the dwellings, with oleanders, acacias, eucalyptuses and oaks suggesting wild abandon beyond."

above *The 134 Freeway and lights from the historic Colorado Street Bridge beyond provide a supernatural backdrop to this refuge under the bridges.*

Photography by Anthony Peres

Carol Soucek King Author/Design Journalist

above *Bouquets of fountain grass volunteer whimsical offerings along one of the property's three old stone walls, while jubilantly blooming oleanders celebrate summer six months of the year.*

right *At the master bedroom's entry, silver dollar eucalyptuses, acacias and pyracanthas soften the view of the bridge without completely concealing its drama.*

above *Railroad ties descend through wild cherry trees and California oaks to the gazebo and a giant eucalyptus beyond.*

left *Added fifteen years after the main house was built, the gazebo's stained red cedar platform floats amid eucalyptuses and overlooks the creek. The structure's one wall is of river rock found on the property.*

above *The author with Gypsy: "With such boulders for seating as well as contemplation, who needs chairs?"*

left *Ascending from the gazebo, railroad ties weave through a tunnel of native California oaks. The stone walls, found on the property, are thought to have been built at the turn of the century, when this path led to a mill in the creek below.*

opposite *Running south under the freeway toward the Colorado Street Bridge built in 1913, this natural waterway forms the property's eastern border. The area's name is Arroyo Seco, Spanish for "dry gully," except this creek bed is never dry.*

Cactus Cornucopia

"April through July is spectacular at Rancho Diablo, our home in Lafayette, California, with more than fifty varieties of cactuses in vivid, large-scale flower. Especially since cactus flowers are often short-lived — developing slowly, opening quickly, then fading within a couple of days — we consider each bloom an event.

"The cactus garden, which we designed in conjunction with Margaret Majua, contributes to the Old California temperament of our restored 1930s-era Monterey-style house. It is classically drought-tolerant, which means it is intolerant of soggy soil as well. Before planting, the site was prepared with rock and loose, specially designed soil to insure free drainage. Still, cactuses seem unusually 'intelligent' for plants and often can adapt to cold and wet weather and even right themselves after shifting in soft ground. They seem to stay out of each other's way and will grow away from the sun to avoid becoming entangled.

"It is mildly perilous to tend a cactus garden. Sharp, sometimes venomous spines make their way through leather gloves and the thickest clothing. Still, the spectacle of a cactus garden, saturated with flowers ablaze on a summer afternoon, causes the memory of this injustice to fade."

Lucia Howard Architect

David Weingarten Architect

above *New cactuses, selected for cold-hardiness, are mostly of Peruvian extraction. Now rain and cold provoke anxiety, but astonishingly little damage.*

opposite *The huge wisteria shading the two-story porch is probably the same vintage as the sixty-seven-year-old house.*

Photography by Alan Weintraub

below *Extending beyond the porch, the sandstone terrace points toward Mt. Diablo in the distance. The house is named Rancho Diablo in its honor. On the terrace, a table and chairs constructed of a friend's horses' shoes are more comfortable than they appear.*

above *"The short history of our garden has been eventful," say Lucia Howard and David Weingarten, principals of Ace Architects who, with garden designer Margaret Majua, planned their home's outdoor environment. "In the first winter, half the cactuses were lost to our worst freeze in one hundred years."*

left *Cactuses and succulents often have a startling scale. The "giant artichoke" agave and the huge flowers on the various tiny cactuses seem closer to prehistoric than to contemporary plants.*

opposite *The cool, dark porch allows people to survive the southwest exposure that is perfectly fit for cactuses.*

Reclaiming Nature

"My firm, The Landmark Group, specializes in resort planning, and in the mid-60s we were best known for our 'natural' swimming pools and waterways, all of which influenced the design of my former garden in Brisbane, Australia.

"Set on five acres, the garden surrounds a house I constructed of recycled porphyry stone, beams, bricks and slate and which itself is an intricate part of my holistic approach to the entire site. Timber verandas integrate into the garden, which includes rainforest, aquatic plants and open lawns.

"A creek runs through the bottom of the garden. The natural swimming pool has been integrated into this area with a man-made natural stream/waterwall coming down from the house. Also located beside the pool is a studio that was our original office, which was a creative environment in which to design. The original property was farmland with only one tree remaining on the property. Over a period of eleven years, with all the varying foliage and water, it has attracted some fifty species of birds."

above *The grounds include a mix of aquatic plants, waterlilies and other species native to the location. The goal was to re-create what might have been here before the land was cleared at the turn of the century for use as a dairy farm.*

Photography courtesy of Donald Monger

Donald Monger Landscape Architect

above *Donald Monger at the main house, whose interior and exterior he integrated by using the same demolition materials throughout — timber beams, slate and porphyry stone from the old Brisbane courthouse.*

above *The studio's veranda, built out over the swimming pool, seems at one with the surrounding vegetation — bottlebrush, paper bark, lomandra grass and gray gum eucalyptus trees — all of which are native to the area.*

left *The pool's "natural" attributes include cantilevered railroad ties, sandstone boulders ramped so bathers can walk right into the water, more boulders arranged in a multitude of shallow sitting areas ... and a diving log!*

Complete Harmony

"I have always called my design 'garden wall architecture.' It is design that is sensitive to site and climate; that includes natural light, human scale, simplicity of materials and forms used indoors and out; that dissolves the building into the site and brings the site into the heart of the building.

"For my family's beachfront home in Malibu, California, I designed a wood platform raised over the water to be used as a garden inside and out, erasing any distinction between exterior and interior. Landscape elements are integrated into the architecture with wood lattice used as arbors and windows and as railings and walls. At our Santa Monica home, a sparse, drought-tolerant, tactile Southern California landscape reinforces a paved abstract plane that reaches to the canyon and mountains beyond. It provides a front-row seat for an ever-changing show of clouds and sunsets. For Goldman Firth Boccato's office building in Malibu, native drought-tolerant landscape was researched and selected to complement the architecture's colors and textures and to emphasize its proximity to ocean and mountains.

"I have a visceral reaction to a garden's textures, colors, sounds and reflectivity. Every aspect represents to me a psychological, spiritual and artistic link."

Ron Goldman Architect

above *Cactus, garlic and liriope mingle with bright red patio furniture to celebrate the water-filled "backyard" of the Goldmans' Malibu residence.*

above left *The terraced entry becomes a sculpture garden of potted plants. The purple plum and floating stairs create a dance of shadows on the white plaster walls.*

above right *A trellised bay window extends the family room into the outdoor garden. The pink wall screens the road and provides a connection to the natural hillside garden beyond.*

left *A lattice-covered entry path leads to the front door, while potted plants informally stand guard. The soft texture of the leaves contrasts with the starkness of the walls.*

Photography by Glen Allison, except above left by Ron Goldman

right *At the Goldman Firth Boccato office gray-green and blue leaves of the multiheaded yucca rostrada and eucalyptus trees complement and blend with the natural colors and materials of the architecture. The blue-green tint in the glass reflects the ocean and coastal terrace environment.*

Photography by Tom Bonner

left *Ron Goldman under a stainless steel trellis in front of his architectural offices.*

Photography by Undine Prohl

below *A village of simple industrial forms and materials sits in a park of eucalyptus trees and opuntia prickly pear cactus.*

Photography by Ron Goldman

above *The rhythmic stockade of stucco columns at the Santa Monica house stands as a symbolic gateway leading to the canyon below. Bronze flax and bougainvillea are silhouetted against the wall of the modern hacienda.*

Photography by Undine Prohl

right *In the entry court, a rainchain carries water into a pond of gravel surrounded by bamboo and kangaroo paws. The sound of bubbling water masks the noise of the traffic and city outside.*

Photography by Crandall & Crandall

left *The abstract plane of paving reaches to the canyon and mountains beyond, while Adirondack chairs provide front row seats for an ever-changing theater of clouds and sunsets.*

Photography by Marvin Rand

below *The narrow entrance leads through a grove of bamboo into a minimalist oasis. Walls, plantings, colors and textures provide the tranquility of a "natural" Mondrian setting.*

Photography by Undine Prohl

A Creative Oasis

"My garden in Los Angeles is both laboratory and sculpture studio. I test properties and qualities of scale, materials, forms and perceptions.

"The garden has evolved along with my practice and is composed of various elements of my theoretical and built work. Designed in collaboration with my husband Michael Lehrer, an architect, the various spaces function as play and outdoor dining areas and, in Renaissance style, extend to the larger landscape through 'borrowed' views.

"The perception of the front garden is a traditional American suburban front yard with standard planting and white picket fence. The presence of a colossal urn poses questions of scale and origin.

"From the street, a silver stairway leads to a terrace of crushed recycled glass at the base of the house, its shimmering pebbles reflecting sunlight in ever-changing panels of color. At night, they catch the evening sky in a sparkling inversion.

"The rear garden also incorporates reused materials in broken concrete paving and a water wall. The small square fountain is a miniaturization of traditional Islamic water gardens. The tropical palms and bougainvillea are inspired by my childhood in Central America.

"My garden is the place where I can exercise my greatest freedom in design."

above left *Like a stage set, the composition of the front garden terrace recalls more familiar forms.*

above right *The artist in her garden.*

opposite *The traditional American front yard is re-presented through subtle plays on form, color and scale.*

Photography by Jay Venezia

Mia Lehrer Landscape Architect

Urban but Wild

Seattle, *Washington*

"Two small urban rooftop gardens adjoin our condominium in Seattle's Pioneer Square Historic District. To us, these gardens, which are formally laid out but casual in their execution, suggest the wild but urban character we were after.

"While most of the residences Olson Sundberg creates for clients are rather grand in scale, my own garden is much smaller and more eccentric. Still, there is a similarity in the integration of plant materials and garden spaces into the overall architectural theme. Here, that theme is the city, its buildings acting as garden sculptures.

"My wife Katherine works in the larger garden on the north terrace facing downtown Seattle. She loves to garden and to experiment with various annuals and perennials as well as with colors that relate to the historic buildings nearby. On the south terrace off our bedroom is my tiny garden, in which I find a Zen-like tranquility.

"For both Katherine and me, as well as for the people on the street who smile when they look up at these refreshing green spots in the middle of the city, our rooftop gardens bring a nurturing sense of warmth, life and softness to the urban setting."

above *The historic Smith Tower, once the tallest building west of the Mississippi River, seems like a piece of garden sculpture.*

James W. P. Olson Architect

Photography by Michael Jensen

overleaf *Architect James Olson, principal of Olson Sundberg Architects, surveys Seattle from his urban oasis in the center of the Pioneer Square Historic District. The hedge is privet, and clematis climbs on the trellis above.*

below *At the south terrace, Boston and English ivies and Virginia creeper, all chosen for ease of maintenance, are joined by shade-loving impatiens, whose color almost exactly matches the historic buildings beyond.*

above *Beyond the kitchen, the north terrace offers a verdant view of African daisies, cosmos, Marguerite daisies and lobelia, all of which are annuals and have been selected to relate to the urban colors.*

A Bagel Garden

"This typical Georgian row house in Boston, Massachusetts, bore the square hedge remnants of a former garden. The garden I installed when I lived there was temporary — providing the opportunity for experimentation.

"Meant to be humorous and ironic, and contrasting formal French garden design with more contemporary materials, the garden juxtaposed the homey nature of the bagel with the formal arrangement and elite connotations of the color purple. A *petite parterre embroiderie* was set within the existing hedges — two concentric Italianate squares of 16-inch-high boxwoods. Between inner and outer squares is a purple gravel strip, upon which sits a point grid of ninety-six weatherproofed bagels. Inside the hedge's inner square, thirty purple floss flowers were planted in rows of six, reversing the purple color pattern.

"Contextually, this domestic material seems funny and a bit out of place in staunchly traditional Back Bay Boston. Yet it was also designed to look beautiful, picking up the colors of the sidewalk and existing Japanese maple."

Boston, *Massachusetts*

above *Strolling down Boston's Marlborough Street, one can discover many a gardener's fancies by peering behind fences. But a walkway strewn with bagels?*

Martha Schwartz Landscape Architect/Artist

Photography by Alan Ward

46

above *The colors of the purple gravel and green boxwood hedges correspond to the hues of the Japanese maple that hovers above the garden.*

above *The contrast of a formal garden's geometry with the domestic nature of bagels demands thoughtful contemplation — and what better function has a garden than that?*

left *Martha Schwartz on "Why a Bagel Garden?": "The garden was intended as a celebration as well as a commentary on the state of the profession of landscape architecture."*

*Photography left
Martha Schwartz, Inc.*

ROMANTICISTS

Native Ranch Style   Outdoor Rooms   Town House Retreat

Harmonious Grounds   Traditional Tropics

A Natural Balance   Bungalow Setting   Rambling Hillside

A Country Retreat   Prairie Home Garden   Garden Labyrinth

Cherished Sanctuary   Rooftop Haven

Native Ranch Style

"It was extremely important to me that I create a peaceful atmosphere that my husband and I could enjoy year-round. At Pine Tree Lake Ranch in Mountain Center, California, with its lakes, its magnificent boulder formations, in which we occasionally find mortars left long ago by the Cahuilla Indians, and its high elevation in the San Jacinto Mountains encouraging nature's vivid response to the seasons, we find serenity every minute we are there.

"The garden that surrounds the home, loosely based on a Cliff May ranch-style house, was designed to enhance the property's natural beauty and to soften the architecture with indigenous greenery and flowers, portions of which are viewed from every window. As lush and elegant as those designed for my clients, yet relaxed and seemingly uncalculated, the garden at our ranch also had to be conducive to the elements, from harsh winters to drought-like late summers and falls. Thus, the blankets of flowers, both wild and planted, are joined by Ponderosa pine, Douglas fir, live oak, birch, manzanita and other chaparral.

"All evoke a vitality and energy that I find extremely stimulating. For me, as a designer, one of the greatest pleasures of the garden is in the visualization."

above *Every attempt was made to utilize indigenous plants and boulder formations in planning the home and property, including the entrance designed around existing horticulture.*

Photography by Anthony Peres

Erika Brunson Interior Designer

above *The antique gate located in a whitewashed wall leads beyond to the property's wilderness perimeter — including the coyotes, raccoons, squirrels and even mountain lions who call the San Jacinto wilderness home.*

right *When planning the landscaping of the ranch, Erika Brunson opted for manicured lawns, particularly around the pool, which is also surrounded by pine trees, rock formations and flowers that, for the most part, are native to the region.*

51

above *One of the property's three man-made lakes fed by seasonal springs and streams and stocked with bass, trout and catfish. The lake is surrounded by pine trees, flowering plums and birch trees as well as wildflowers.*

right *"There are trails for riding on the ranch as well as miles of trails available for riding in the surrounding area." — Erika Brunson on one of her favorite Arabians.*

left *The pool heightens all of the elements — as well as the view of Mount San Jacinto and Tahquitz Peak, two of the highest peaks in the San Jacinto range.*

overleaf *The southerly view facing Rouse Ridge and Thomas Mountain includes boulder formations, native grasses and manicured lawns — punctuated by the stately Ponderosa pines. The house and tower can be seen through the trees.*

Outdoor Rooms

"When my husband and I moved to our property in Malibu Canyon, I lived with it for almost a year without changing anything, save for trimming the existing vines and bushes and planting herbs for cooking. I simply wanted to feel the pulse of my particular piece of earth.

"Later, as time and money allowed, I created many outdoor rooms — dining areas, cozy nooks for reading and relaxing, a separate summer house/garden cottage — as well as wild cutting gardens, vegetable gardens, a field of lavender and many beds filled with herbs, flowers and perennials.

"A country garden with formal touches, its inspiration is drawn from the many places I have visited and photographed. The result is a personal collection of memories and moods.

"Being in California, the garden is able to be an extension of the home — ideal for my preference for breaking up space and an idea I carry into my clients' gardens also. In addition, the sounds of birds and water make these outdoor rooms multidimensional.

"My goal was to create a rejuvenating oasis. It provides breathing space for further creativity and keeps me grounded with nature's peacefulness — to me, the *true* reality."

above *The old arbor is hand-painted and framed by spiral-shaped junipers with artemisia Powis Castle at their base. Beyond is a field of lavender, small Mexican evening primrose bushes, a wisteria vine and towering yellow verbascum.*

*Photography by
Karen Dominguez Brann*

Karen Dominguez Brann Landscape Designer

above *This perennial garden was created around a flagstone table. It is packed to overflowing with fever-few, summer lilac, orchid rockrose,* Lavatera bicolor *and "Iceberg" roses. The birds attracted to the feeder add the sound and motion.*

right *Nestled in a field of mustard is the original barn, built in 1880.*

Photography by
Karen Dominguez Brann

bottom right *Karen Dominguez Brann — "I believe one's garden should be a reflection of one's personal vision."*

Photography by Edy Owen

Town House Retreat

"Being a residential interior designer, I am especially concerned about the relationship between garden, structure and interior. The scope and style of my own garden, created with my design associate David Graham, are completely interrelated to the restrictions of the long narrow space outside our Los Angeles town house and the environment established within. It demanded a semi-traditional style — organized and relying on form and scale without being too formal.

"This approach allowed us much variety. There are azalea trees plus potted plants for changeable color and form. Ficus, camellias and ivy create a backdrop for conversation; plum trees and magnolias gather protectively around diners. Begonias, impatiens, caladiums and variegated pittosporums bring pastels to a seasonal planting bed. Hanging baskets teeming with blooms and staggered in height add visual impact and work with the trellis. A large, iron Belle Epoque fountain, wire topiary frames (left bare to accent their sense of architecture), other statuary and used brick reflect the interior's old-world aspects.

"We do all the gardening ourselves, learning from nature what should be grown, molded and pruned to create the peaceful, verdant setting we desire."

above *A large French fountain, wire topiary frames, recycled brick, and garden statuary carry the interior's old-world environment out to the water garden.*

Photography by Charles S. White

Ron Hefler Interior Designer

left *"We use the garden daily for dining and meeting with our clients."— Ron Hefler, right, with design associate David Graham.*

above *In the garden's dining area, spring flowering plum trees, magnolias, azaleas and flowering annuals combined with used brick create a soft, dappled, sunlit retreat.*

right *The conversation area is lush with evergreen plantings — ficus, camellias and ivy — creating a soft green backdrop for summer entertaining and, throughout the year, accents of seasonal color.*

Harmonious Grounds

Shelter Island, New York

"When we moved into our eighteenth-century house on Shelter Island, New York, we established our business there, too, as The Homestead Garden & Design Collaborative. While Dale continues as partner in the architecture firm, Bates & Booher, The Collaborative allows us to design homes and gardens together, with our own home as an ongoing example of our collaborative efforts. And gardens never really end. Day to day, season to season, they are constant balancing acts between the mind and the eye.

"From the first, we worked as a team, side by side scooping out the swampland and making a pond hemmed in with iris. As I was dreaming of the gardens that would flourish around the house, Dale was updating it inside with plumbing and electricity. While I was planting roses and planning borders, sketching a stone wall between border and lawn and commencing the privet hedge for privacy, Dale was building pergolas, gates, a grape arbor to frame one ancient shed and converting another into the pool pavilion — all painted green to fit easily into the landscape. Whether made by man or by nature, our goal was to create a sense of unpretentious intimacy that would harmonize with the original cottage."

above *A protective fence keeps deer on this side of the vegetable garden.*

opposite *A row of Adirondack rockers provides a gentle resting place.*

Photography by Mick Hales

Dale Booher Architect/Planner

Lisa Stamm Landscape Designer

left *Dale Booher with Lisa Stamm, against a backdrop of "Betty Prior" roses. "Designing pergolas and gates for gardens — now that, to me, seems the height of architecture!"*

below *The emerald-green leaves and amethyst-colored flowers of lacecap hydrangea bestow on the garden a treasure trove of jewel-like hues.*

left *The serendipitous look of the perennial border derives from an abundance of informally planted species, including iris, peonies, nepeta, lythrum, meadow rue and New England astors.*

above *Meandering paths and the lawn's gentle elevations make the property on the south side of the home appear endless.*

right *Beneath an arbor built by Dale Booher, the border planted by Lisa Stamm presents a view that could stir one's reveries throughout the day.*

Traditional Tropics

"In a rainforest high atop Tantalus Mountain overlooking Honolulu, Hawaii, my garden is both traditional and tropical. Landscape architect Steve Mechler divided the property into a casual arrangement of terraces and outdoor rooms, framing every view from the house with lush nature. There is the shade garden, the impatiens garden, the lower terrace and lily pond, the dog yard, the anthurium walk, the clivia circle, the bamboo forest .... The fragrant white garden, where we entertain, is filled with jasmine, gardenias, honeysuckle and lilies. And everywhere orchids are perched in trees for optimal growing conditions as well as viewing.

"The result is floral, colorful — a carbon copy of my interior design and its unexpected mixtures. From its enchanting dawns to its magically illuminated nights, it brings wonder and contentment to my life. Also, especially now that I am a flower arrangement judge for the Garden Club of America, cutting bouquets and creating floral arrangements are priorities. Even though just 'chopping back' is almost a full-time job in this climate, my husband and I both love to garden.

" *The Secret Garden* was probably my favorite childhood book and unconsciously I have tried to create the same fantasy in real life."

above *The jacaranda tree in front of the kitchen conservatory corresponds to the periwinkle exterior.*

Photography by Augie Salbosa

opposite *An overview showing the gazebo with antique French faience dove finial and terraces tucked into the dense greenery of Italian cypress, an oak tree and white begonias. The garden is now part of the Smithsonian's archives of American gardens.*

Allison Holland Interior Designer

Photography by David Livingston

above *Allison Holland, Garden Club of America judge, doing her favorite thing — picking flowers from her garden to create arrangements for her house.*

Photography by Augie Salbosa

opposite *One of four latticed arches used in the Hollands' daughter's wedding, now relocated in the garden with its azaleas and begonias as well as lilies and mandevilla vine beyond.*

Photography by David Livingston

A Natural Balance

"At each of our homes, it is evident that our gardens reflect the intent of the architecture as well as an appropriateness for the given climate. The Southern Italian influence dictates our Beverly Hills residence. Surrounded by a forest of evergreen trees, the home is terraced on all sides. Each terrace has its own focal point, such as the pool seen through the living room trellis covered in trumpet vines and bougainvillea. Here, a combination of potted citrus, white azaleas, red geraniums and red epidendrum orchids flanks the colonnade. The hardscape is Santa Rita stone, and the low walls surrounding the terraces are stacked with hand-chiseled stone — all consistent with the architectural style.

"At our Palm Springs residence, lush exotic and tropical plants similar to those found in North Africa and South America surround our 1928 Spanish Colonial-style compound. Mexican and Italian pots overflow with roses, geraniums and oleanders of coral, pink and ivory. A koi pond flowers with waterlilies, papyrus and lotus. Wild green parrots fly among the date palms as the jacaranda trees softly drop their lavender leaves — all in harmony with the architecture and climate."

above *The pool at the Palm Springs residence, set among a grove of date palms with a majestic backdrop of the San Jacinto Mountains, establishes the exotic mood.*

Photography by Mary E. Nichols

Illya Hendrix Interior Designer

Thomas Allardyce Interior Designer

above *In the Palm Springs home's converted stable, the playful antics of fancy koi and the music of cascading water enhance candlelit dinners.*

Photography by Mary E. Nichols

left *Ilya Hendrix, left, and Thomas Allardyce, in their Beverly Hills garden.*

Photography by Douglas Piburn

Bungalow Setting

Los Angeles, *California*

"As I am a second-generation Angeleno, my city's roots are very important to me and, in planning the garden for our Spanish-style bungalow, I wanted to create a magical outdoor space my family and friends could enjoy that would also reflect Los Angeles's history. This I achieved primarily by making use of period materials.

"Sandstone pathways, inappropriate to the garden of one period house, was transferred to my own garden. When the Beverly Hills Hotel closed for renovation, I eagerly acquired as much of that landmark's old cast-iron furniture as I could for our outdoor seating. After the last earthquake, I found several fallen chimney flues that I installed as planters and filled with an informal, unstructured mix similar to our bed of roses, hydrangeas, tomatoes and herbs. The only new items in my garden are the reproductions of historic Malibu tiles made today by California Pottery that I used to detail step risers and the fish pond.

"We use our garden all year long, beginning each day with having our coffee there. Also, because it is such an unusual urban space, it attracts neighborhood children for whom the pond has become an unofficial watering hole. For us, that *is* magic."

Lory Johansson Interior Designer

above *The rear garden wall, covered with creeping fig, serves as a privacy wall and also provides a focal point as guests enter the garden from the right. Molly, a whippet, is ever present. The path is made of Arizona flagstone taken from another residence where it was not so appropriate.*

Photography by Douglas Hill

left *"The sound of moving water adds a further note of tranquility and acts as white noise, canceling out disturbing urban noise."* — Lory Johansson, partner with June Robinson in Ergo Design Works.

Photography by Kenneth Johansson

above *The pond is integrated colored plaster, which the designer prefers for its fresco-like appearance. The water cascades from a lion's head into a basin filled with her daughter's seashell collection. Within the pond are purple water hyacinth, pink water canna and a yellow waterlily. An "Angel's Face" rose climbs the wall.*

Photography by Douglas Hill

Rambling Hillside

"Our garden rambles over three-and-a-half acres of hillside in Santa Barbara's picturesque Hope Ranch and includes a small evergreen orchard of citrus and avocado trees with backdrops of the Pacific Ocean and the Santa Ynez Mountains. Even the flower gardens spread out naturally, accessed by pathways from one hillside through another and complementing our house with color. The colors of the hardscape, buff crushed rock interspersed with stepped, gray-brown railroad ties, complement the Saltillo tile decks and buff Norman brick as well. To reach the guest house and its gardens, we planned winding paths through Monterey pines, magnolia, oak and Hawaiian orchid trees.

"Seasonal flowers provide full color year-round at both houses, and even my favorite, the rose — I have approximately 180 rose bushes! — blooms in Santa Barbara ten months of the year. So our garden's flowers fill our home always. In addition, the art throughout our home's interior reflects my devotion to our gardens, with most of my commissions being of gardens and florals by local artists.

"Inside or outside, my gardens are near and, surrounded by the peace and pleasure they offer, I feel closer to what's important in life than any place else on earth."

above *One of the property's four rose gardens — each bordered by miniature roses, hybrid tea roses, floribunda and antique English roses — that rise across rolling lawns and groups of white birch trees.*

Photography by Jerome Adamstein

Mabel Shults Interior Designer

right *The guest house is nestled among Monterey pines, grandiflora oleander, orchid trees, magnolias and live oak trees.*

above *Mabel Shults, at her home's lower-level entry terrace, stands among boldly planted clay pots surrounding solanum and tall fuschia shrubs. On the upper level, copper pots are planted with ficus surrounded by pansies.*

right *Alongside the guest house terraces, the gardens combine elements of light and shade with form, texture and color in uniting gardens and buildings. More than twenty seasonal flowers — including hybrid bearded iris, gladiolas, day lilies, shasta daisies and calla lilies — provide color year-round.*

A Country Retreat

"Within my 110 acres in Garrison, New York, I designed ten as a garden within an existing context of mature hemlocks, white birches, oaks, maples and pines. The resulting style was achieved less by adding than by editing — removing some trees and trimming others to allow the trunks to express themselves. In addition, I created a 3.2-acre lake by constructing a dam at an existing spring and brook. For color, I arrange potted plants of seasonal flowers in areas close to the house.

"It is such a simple plan. Yet it does reflect the type of work I do for clients in that I always base my design decisions on the context of the situation — and here the context was the completely natural environment.

"And I must say I do love it here. I dine outside. I have a tent I purchased in Morocco, enabling me to serve even large parties outside. I swim in the lake. I even do my own light gardening. To me, being in this garden is like a Zen experience, a retreat from all the craziness of the city and the rigors of running Juan Montoya Design Corporation."

above *Fall is one of the most glorious times at this country home, where, rather than planting more, Juan Montoya chose to simply edit the property's existing trees, thus depending on them for color as well as form.*

Photography by Durston Saylor

Photography (above and page 81) by Jaime Ardiles-Arce

Juan Montoya Interior Designer

left *Juan Montoya with his vintage Porsche at the end of his home's approach of crushed gravel, which he prefers over poured concrete in natural settings. The cobblestone terraces, situated so as to overlook the lake, are ample enough for entertaining as well as for parking.*

above *The protected terrace adjacent to the dining area extends the home's indoor/outdoor quality and emphasizes the oneness with nature that the designer intended for his home in the woods.*

above *Juan Montoya purchased this Moroccan tent and carpet while on a trip to Marrakesh and now sets it lakeside during good weather. "We virtually never dine inside when we can be here," he says.*

above *Montoya enlarged the existing spring-fed lake and stocked it with fish and a snapping turtle — "to be avoided at all costs while swimming!" he says.*

above *The dam and waterfall, designed to keep the lake fresh for swimming and canoeing, provide the equally important sense of movement and sound. Located near the driveway's last curving approach to the house, they introduce a kinetic and aural energy suggesting a rite of passage into a sacred naturescape.*

right *When the season turns wintry, the lake becomes a sculpture frozen in space and time. Rather than create a direct, grand approach, the driveway was purposefully allowed to meander naturally along the lake's edge, thereby preserving trees and the natural rise and fall of the land.*

Prairie Home Garden

Champaign, Illinois

"Both our house and garden, incongruously adjacent to the University of Illinois's concrete complex on the flat prairies of Champaign, exude a cozy, cottage-like feeling. The garden continues the interior's American country collectibles with antique urns, pots, wire baskets and antique signage. The hand-crafted willow teahouse and patio area and the fencing and convivial gathering of topiaries further support our respect for the past as well as all visual entrancements.

"Designing our own garden, we have been more adventurous than clients often permit. We even try plants not tested in this area and mix them with other appealing elements found while traveling. We also devote luxurious doses of attention to the seasons, watching our more than four thousand bulbs bloom in the spring, producing a galaxy of perennials in the summer, encouraging richly textured and colorful plants in the fall and, in the winter, filling our snow-covered willow teahouse with a lighted Christmas tree.

"We enjoy our pocket of nature daily — nights of entertaining, followed by mornings alone pruning and planting, and then, when passersby stop to look at what we have created, we invite them in — once again filling our garden with festivity."

above *The bungalow is situated behind a tailored front yard highlighted with* Shirobana spiraea, *dwarf Alberta spruce and red twig dogwood along the New York bluestone walk. The steps are flanked with boxwood.*

Photography by Dave Weaver, Jr.

Scott Larimer Landscape Designer
Rick Orr Floral Designer

left A house for purple martins sits amid its own paradise of a peegee hydrangea, maiden grass, feverfew, purple coneflower, lavender, trumpet vine, evergreen candytuft, a Persian lilac tree and an old-fashioned rose.

above "Our garden reflects our personalities. It is an extension of our beings." — Scott Larimer, right, with Rick Orr.

right Adjoining the willow teahouse is a water feature that Scott Larimer designed, of New York granite on two levels. Within the pools, koi mingle with various water plants, while from the edge, amid crepe myrtle, ferns and boxwood, a 1920s concrete turtle looks on.

Garden Labyrinth

"In our small garden space in Norman, Oklahoma, we created mystery. Paths offer several routes, over lawn or through groves, under rose arches or through hydrangeas, past sun-loving Mediterranean plants or shaded rhododendrons and azaleas. Our climate, on the edge of many zones, invites experiments, and this garden quickly changes costumes, moods and light.

"Nostalgia and history are companions along the way. Recollections include classical parterres in a boxwood hedge, 1920s Pasadena borders in a burst of Florence Yoch's favorite tulip, "Clara Butt," eighteenth-century England in a lawn within a gathering of trees, April in Paris in wisteria over a walk focused on a Parisian dormer.

"Surprises subvert patterns in the garden. Plants express their own character, and artifacts recall friends. Lilies poke through the box hedges, a historic stone face leers out from a bed of ivy, ajuga wanders from its bed onto the lawn. The design invites a taste for unravelling, for recognizing layers of meanings.

"As in fabled labyrinths, the reward for adventures of mind and foot is the comfort of repose and companionship. Benches and a table offer welcoming respites in this place far removed from the rush of contemporary life."

above *The Rose Walk beckons with China rose "Madame Alfred Carrière," hybrid musk roses "Cornelia" and "Prosperity," rugosa rose "Hansa," along with "Fred Loads" and the "Yellow Rose of Texas."*

James J. Yoch Landscape Designer

Photography by James J. Yoch

above *The beflowered brick terrace, with an olive jar that is now a fountain alongside a welcoming dining area, is used sunup to sundown for entertainment, study, the professor's classes and, adds Yoch, "idleness and daydreaming."*

right *James J. Yoch, landscape designer, professor of Shakespearean literature — and artist — sketching amid the lilies on an unbelievably hot day.*

Cherished Sanctuary

"Sir Robert Lorimer wrote, 'A garden is a sort of sanctuary, a chamber roofed by heaven, to wander in, to cherish, to dream through undisturbed ...' Our garden on Long Island, New York, a deeply satisfying experience of color, shape, texture, smell and renewal of life, evokes a similar response. It is a dialogue as important as music, poetry and art. We share it with all sorts of wildlife and the camaraderie of other gardeners.

"Creating our garden has been a slow, hands-on evolution. Influenced by childhood memories, other gardens and great expectations, we also wanted the garden to be an extension of the house and to relate to its proportions. To give protection from winds, we planted hedges that became walls. Plants were chosen for structure or the garden's bones. We designed architectural elements, such as grape arbors and see-through fences. We played with paving patterns. We respected our surroundings, local traditions, native plants; we observed light and shade.

"By now our garden is a series of small outdoor chambers, each a composition of its own. The garden cannot be seen all at once, and it gives great pleasure as you pass from room to room, mysteries around every corner."

above *The entrance court, shown in spring, leads the eye beyond the privet hedge, flanked by locust trees underplanted with* Helleborus foetidus *and narcissus.*

Photography by Erika R. Shank

William & Erika Shank Architectural Interior Designers

left *Seen in the fall, the blue Atlas cedar, trained over an arbor, provides a cool contrast to the sycamore maple's golden hues beyond.*

above *The trellis forms a dramatic proscenium arch, while tall, stately spires of white foxglove take front stage center.*

right *Viewed from above in the spring, the White Garden presents a tapestry of green and white foliage around the pool. Influenced by a Palladian window, the garden's structure is created with American arborvitae. The beds are edged in clipped boxwood with variegated boxwood accenting the corners.*

right *"New Dawn" roses cover the arbor in June, while native inkberry holly marks the four corners of the sundial garden.*

below *Waterlilies, lotus and variegated reeds seemingly grow amid clouds as well as water in the reflecting pool, shown here in spring. Edging the pond are reticulata irises.*

left *"My interest in landscape photography started primarily by the making of our own garden." — Architectural interior designer Erika R. Shank, whose photographic images have by now been widely published.*

above *Shown in early fall, the front garden's grassy path looks west toward the Memorial Garden, where staddle stones, washed by the morning's first light, can be seen through rose-covered arches. Ageratum and Pennisetum alopecuroides prolong the flowering season and soften the brick edges.*

Rooftop Haven

"Mies van der Rohe's 'less is more' philosophy is a major theme throughout my design — except in my own garden, my rooftop garden on the Hudson River in New York City's Tribeca neighborhood. This, my private refuge following busy workdays, I had to have lush, almost over-planted. It also had to feel easy and comfortable — like the beach, but with a formal touch.

"Los Angeles landscape designer William Shapiro helped select the ingredients. Casual notes came in the form of Long Island daisies, black-eyed Susans and beach grasses, which withstand heat and cold and, most important, the river area's strong winds ... they also make a wonderful sound in the breeze. Formal accents were English ivy, roses, classical urns, the fragrant boxwood in planters with painted designs reminiscent of Italian flags. For additional color and texture, we chose euonymus and veronica.

"For me the garden serves mainly as a place to relax. Gardening itself is the most restful activity I do. It gives me reason to shop all the nurseries on Long Island's east end. Then, what could be more pleasant than sitting down with a glass of wine and watching the river and ships go by?"

David Walker Interior Designer

above *The small, roofed penthouse with a wooden gridwork reflects the changes of the season as wisteria loses its leaves, exposing the mums and holly bushes aligning the rectangular structure. The seating upholstery and bracket are of much warmer coloration in order to blend with all seasons.*

Photography by Peter Vitale

right *Miniature pink climbing roses and English ivy cascade over a nineteenth-century terra-cotta urn. Deep-purple statice fills a concrete urn with a Mayan relief.*

above *"Retreating to my rooftop hideaway is the ideal end to a hectic day." — David Walker*

left *Blue Bahia stone mirrors the sky and water as luncheon is set on simple blue-and-yellow ceramic dishes, before the cityscape.*

INTERPRETERS

Wine Country Vistas   Cloistered Classic   Terrace Style

Hillside Rhapsody   Urban Color   Courtyard Garden

European Reflections   Nature Reinvented   Organized Abandon

A Challenging Site   Lush Informality   Japanese Imprint

Cottage Garden   Mediterranean Style

Wine Country Vistas

"The gardens of my two homes in Napa Valley, California, are opposites — a greenscape versus a hardscape. In the first, Bella Oaks (page 97), I was able to use an abundance of perennials, allowing me to weave together some nice relationships of color, texture and fragrance. Various grasses soften the pool, concealing the steps. It is an Italian farmhouse style of planting, a feminine, soft approach that my clients usually prefer.

"At my current house, the garden is as stylized as a contemporary abstract painting, with a sculptured, clean-lined hardscape, not plant materials, defining outdoor rooms. The walls themselves vary in height according to a strict geometric ratio and provide dramatic entries, enclosures and backgrounds for art.

"There is only one variety of tree — and it is a highly sculptural Siouxland poplar that grows into a conical shape. Even the swimming pool, with its three prominent fountains cascading out of another powerfully geometric wall, takes on two functions, with the visual function usually being more important than the play function.

"I am quite enamored with how these walls perform visually at all times. By night they reflect moonlight, and even when days are foggy they continue to project a presence of strength."

above *When viewed from above, the hard-edged sculptural boundaries of the garden are seen as direct extensions of Jack Chandler's current house.*

Photography by Jared Chandler

Jack Chandler Landscape Architect

above *Perennials such as Russian sage, Mexican evening primrose and fountain grass are used in broad sweeps of color that complement the simple lines of the house.*

Photography by Andrew McKinney

right *"The clean, sculptural lines of these walls project a definitive, patrician presence that fascinates me." — Jack Chandler*

Photography by Jared Chandler

left *The sound of water gushing forcefully from spouts evenly spaced along the wall further enlivens the powerful feeling projected by the Barragán-style pool at the Calistoga residence.*

Photography by Andrew McKinney

above *A heron lifts off from Jack Chandler's sculpture,* Ghost Dock, *which floats in the pond and is driven by the wind.*

Photography by Jared Chandler

right *At the Bella Oaks garden, a pole structure provides a shaded area from which to contemplate breeze-ruffled fountain grass and the quiet surface of the pool.*

Photography by Andrew McKinney

Cloistered Classic

"My garden opens onto a town park which leads to my office at Princeton, making it easy for me to walk back and forth. So the garden is an integral part of my daily life, enabling me to feel connected to the land.

"The garden's design is circumstantial. I had bought not a conventional house, but a 1926 warehouse, Italianate in design. Over the years it had become a local trash dump, and the neighbors had camouflaged it by growing ivy on its walls. These now wonderfully green walls became the landscape's beginning. I enclosed the garden by adding three more walls, then created a walking border of rice stone, suggested by landscape architect Julie Bargmann, to isolate the central square of grass as a *tapis vert*, or green carpet. Other embellishments include a path to the park, a boxwood hedge bounded by two nineteenth-century English pots at the garden's threshold, eight pollarded sycamores and a terrace of English limestone where a light trellis covered with wisteria imparts a relaxed feeling to the garden's more formal aspects.

"Its privacy, and its sense of continuity with the park as well as with the house, allow me to use my garden fully and to enjoy the sense of place that living on the land provides."

above *On one wall in the forecourt, a topiary of climbing red roses creates a grid across the entire face of the house.*

Photography by Mark Fiennes

Michael Graves Architect

above *Four massive square columns define an English limestone terrace and support a light trellis covered with white wisteria.*

Photography courtesy of Michael Graves, Architect

right *"I guess I am one of these people who talk to their plants. I go out and urge them up!" — the architect with Bill, his black Labrador retriever.*

Photography by Marek Bulaj/ Michael Graves, Architect

Terrace Style

"My garden in Tokyo is planned as an outdoor part of the home's overall design. This idea is reflected in all the projects I have designed. Its being an extension of the interior space allows me and my wife to use it year-round, especially in spring and autumn when the weather is nice. Besides, I love to garden.

"For our garden's floor I selected weather-resistant African bongossi wood due to Tokyo's high humidity and large amount of rain. To hide the garage and soften its wall, I used a

sudare, a bamboo screen. For further cover, I selected the deciduous konara tree because its leaves shield the garden from the summer's heat and fall off in winter to allow sunshine into the garden. For the same reason I chose onizuda ivy, which is also deciduous, to cover the lightweight steel-and-glass ceiling. Various types of evergreen ivy serve as ground cover.

"Because of the small lot and relatively small floor plan, this terrace garden is an important part of the living space. The garden's trees and flowers allow us to experience the change of seasons. We derive from it energy, relaxation and the feeling of nature."

Takekuni Ikeda Architect

above *Beneath a protective ceiling of lightweight steel and glass and surrounded by konara trees and various ivies, Dr. and Mrs. Ikeda find refuge in the middle of Tokyo.*

Photography by Shinkenchiku-sha Co. Ltd.

opposite *A* sudare, *or bamboo screen, hides the garage and softens the backdrop of this terrace garden, shielded by deciduous konara trees and onizuda ivy.*

Photography by Tomio Ohashi

Hillside Rhapsody

Los Angeles, *California*

"Even before I purchased this home, with its bleak hillside and cement yard, I used to imagine how I would use water, trees, trellises, lush plantings and year-round color to create a country feeling in busy Los Angeles. It was like writing a book, with each part of the garden a different chapter ... the soothing waterfall, the grotto pavilion ... the embracing trellis ... the topiary fox hunt and rabbit/giraffe tea party ... the three bird chateaux ....

"Just as in the interiors I design, the composition is based on a wide range of impressions garnered through travels. The grotto pavilion alone, inspired by an old European town, is covered with mosses, creeper, miniature Santa Barbara daisies, lobelia and a wealth of unusual little blossoming plants such as purple robe, rock foil and Easter bonnet alyssum. The perspective arched trellis is flanked with ferns and pink and blue hydrangeas, while a climbing rose winds its way around a flowering pear tree in which is perched a bird cottage planted still further with miniature roses and ivies. Stepping-stones are grouted with baby's tears, white Nancy, spotted dead nettle and green stonecrop. Even the names in my garden's collection are to me a rhapsody."

above *A perspective arched trellis is flanked with ferns, mosses, delphiniums, and blue and pink hydrangeas, while a climbing rose winds its way around a flowering pear tree.*

opposite *The grotto pavilion is covered with many varieties of mosses, creepers, miniature Santa Barbara daisies, lobelia, Purple Robe, rockfoil and Easter bonnet alyssum.*

Photography by Charles White

Douglas Pierce Hiatt Interior Designer

left *"I wanted to create a garden in the city that would have the sights and sounds of the country."* — Douglas Pierce Hiatt

below *A life-size giraffe overlooks a rabbit serving tea on a moss-covered table complete with teacups and a twig chair topped by a small birdhouse. The retaining wall offers profuse delights — roses mixed with plumbego and honeysuckle, garlands made of ivy, and even a bird chateau.*

left *Amid white daisies sprinkled with cosmos are two almost life-size horses and riders and three hounds — all pursuing the fox. From beneath a weeping willow tree a field of fuchsias spreads past cascading plumbego and into a collection of old-fashioned English roses.*

Urban Color

"Whether pruning and digging or simply relaxing, we have always seen our garden as a refuge for quiet meditation. Certainly this is true of our property in Charleston, an island gem embedded in a urban setting. This challenging site has two canvases for garden crafting, a front show garden and a rear garden of repose.

"A visual gift to passersby, the front garden fencing is studded with old-fashioned roses and flowering jasmine. Beneath the pickets, soapwort and candytuft spill onto the sidewalk. Palmettos ring the house and bring the garden into the street. A zoysia grass panel edged in glazed bricks and ancient flagstones sets off a fantasy planting of ligularia and blue lacecap hydrangeas beneath a magnolia.

"The rear garden of repose provides a canvas for structural garden experiments. Tall, watery-blue arched walls support curved blue arbors smothered in kiwi and butterfly roses. Beneath the arbors are benches stained pale pink and purple to enliven the garden in the winter. Drizzled-green Chinese egg pots anchor the four corners. A mirrored trellis highlights our 'yard child,' an antique French fountain that radiates pleasure with his surroundings. He has lived in four of our gardens."

above *Seating areas face east or west for summer and winter comfort. Kiwi, akebia and butterfly rose climb the arbor by ironsmith Rick Avrett. The benches, from Smith & Hawken, were stained by the owners.*

Photography by Mary Palmer Dargan

Hugh & Mary Palmer Dargan Landscape Architects

below Hugh and Mary Palmer Dargan with their dogs, Lollipop and Cobby, enjoy the front show garden. The old stone pavers came from an eighteenth-century site nearby and the custom fence was built by carpenter Ray Hamilton. Ligularia and blue lacecap hydrangea bloom beneath the magnolia.

left A vernacular pattern of bluestone and old Charleston brick has been used for the paving court under the arbor. Young akebia and butterfly roses grow up the posts; the festive fabric will be removed after the vines colonize the roof of the arbor.

above The garden's "yard child," a French cast-iron piece, happily resides next to the painted wood wall and mirrored backdrop by ironsmith Rick Avrett.

Courtyard Garden

"Our home in La Canada Flintridge, California, was designed by the late Cliff May, who was known for his ranch-style homes which were inspired by this area's early haciendas built around intimate, sheltered courtyards. Throughout, I have tried to underscore his idea of making the indoors and outdoors become one.

"The extensive interior planting goes right outside with a collection of specimen palms complementary to the architecture and also of the colonial period of Mexico, where we have our second home. There are also seasonal flowers potted for warmth and color that surround the fountain imported from Mexico, its cascading water lending a sense of serenity to the setting. I commissioned a mural to reflect our other home's beach setting on the Sea of Cortez and added an intimate seating area adjacent to the quiet pool and giant bird-of-paradise trees, in pots, to enhance the tropical atmosphere.

"The projects that I create for others are diverse, but I have never had an occasion to create a garden setting such as this. To me it is the ideal expression of California's indoor-outdoor living possibilities, and we do make use of it all year long."

above *A mural reflecting the beachfront setting of the Kinningers' home on the Sea of Cortez in Baja California Sur sets the mood for an intimate seating area adjacent to the quiet pool and its surrounding giant bird-of-paradise trees.*

Photography by Charles White

Linda Merrifield Kinninger Interior Designer

left *"Our property in Mexico is also filled with many varieties of palm, for which we have a personal affection. These palms, as well as the seasonal flowers imported from Mexico, remind us of our other home, which we treasure as well."*
— Linda Merrifield Kinninger

Photography by Bob Bronson
Bronson Photography

below *The hardscape material, chosen by the architect Cliff May, is washed pebble concrete geometric squares with redwood dividers. The fountain, imported from Mexico, provides a focal point from the living room.*

Photography by Charles White

European Reflections

"My garden in East Hampton is a composite of ideas I have collected as an interior designer during my years of travels, when I would photograph and sketch the various gardens I visited. In particular, perhaps reflecting my Italian heritage, I was drawn to the European idea of gardens as rooms. This garden is a collaboration with Elizabeth Lear, a landscape architect who is sensitive to my needs.

"My own garden has become an outdoor room ... four rooms actually ... by fencing and plantings. One is the swimming pool, another the terrace, another the large grassy area opposite the pool and surrounded by rhododendron and, lastly, the grassy area surrounded by bamboo and mountain laurel.

"In addition to the 'rhodies' and mountain laurel, both native to the area, I have used hosta, white hydrangea and ivy, which encircle the pool. The only annuals are the potted geraniums and impatiens. Everything needs a minimum of care.

"To me, these spaces are very serene. They are wonderful for reading, listening to music and dining. I feel very calm there, and the sound of the wind in the pine trees comes close to a religious experience."

above *The original pool was on the opposite side of the garden. This pool was added in 1994 and positioned parallel to the living room so its beauty can be appreciated from the interior; at night, when it is illuminated, the view is especially magical.*

Photography by Erika R. Shank

Michael La Rocca Interior Designer

left *The emphasis in the design of the pool and garden is on balance and serenity. The warm sienna-hued Tennessee Crab Orchard stone that borders the pool on all four sides is itself bordered by beds of ivy.*

below *The terrace as well as the house is constructed completely of cedar that is untreated, thereby allowing nature to take its course and turn the cedar a silver-gray that blends exceptionally well with the garden. The table, of ground marble dust, is reminiscent of tables seen in Roman and Florentine gardens.*

above *The arbor, waiting to be planted with white roses, and the fencing create a welcoming architectural element at the pool area's entry and separate this part of the garden from the more natural setting that surrounds it. Bordering the pool are impatiens, the garden's only annuals, and white hydrangea.*

left *The* Styrax japonicus *planted in the wood terrace is one of four that occur along the home's front facade and which, in spring, are covered with highly fragrant white blossoms with gold centers.*

right *"Form, balance and serenity are the three main ingredients in this garden."* — Michael La Rocca

center *A study in verticality, this view of the garden is composed of strong, decidedly upright forms set in further relief as shafts of sunlight force their way through the trees.*

below *The terrace, which is centered on the garden, looks toward the house and is on an axis with the swimming pool. Adding to the visual enjoyment is the fresh scent of the pines as well as the distinctively natural music they make in the wind.*

Nature Reinvented

"This piece of land in Yautepec, a farming community an hour and a half from Mexico City, used to be an acre of cornfields. Its climatic conditions are extreme, with hot, dry winters and warm, rainy summers. So we had to take an experimental approach to our garden, trying what works and what doesn't. For example, we found that cactuses would rot in the summer and ferns would die in the winter.

"The design emphasized the view toward the Tepozteco Mountains and the creation of pergolas and shady areas. We found it possible to grow within the property's different microclimates a wide variety of plants and trees — more than one hundred kinds of orchids as well as jackfruit, zapotes, bananas, tamarind, papaya and guava. Other design elements are sequence, surprise, spontaneity and organic form. We did not want the garden to look man-made, but rather to express a personal view of nature.

"For an architect to work on his own garden is a mind exercise. A garden can have architectural order, yet it also provides the opportunity to work with an entity that is living, giving to the art of landscape design the magic and mystery of nature itself."

above *A walkway of cuarteron tile with inserts of cobalt blue talavera tile penetrates a field of river stone and points to the focal points — Mexican fan palms, a fountain planted with pineapple and hedera, and a formal circular box hedge beyond. The brick walls are covered with bougainvillea, accented by potted monstera.*

left *"To develop pergolas and shaded areas supporting a wide variety of fragrant plants was one of our goals." — Carlos Pascal, left, and Gerard Pascal.*

Carlos & Gerard Pascal Architects

Photography by Eitan Feinholz

above *The children's pool and sunken pit have been constructed with red brick and cobblestone surrounded by tropical plants, including natal plum, liriope, dwarf date palms and a Mexican fan palm. The organic form of the pool and the arrangement of the plants suggest that nature did this herself!*

above *The intention in the garden was to create a casual and natural environment using plants that thrive in this hot climate, giving it a wild, uncultivated look. The red lava sand path enhances the natural look, and the plants are native to the area.*

opposite *A pond with waterlilies and papyrus is surrounded by a path of rocks set in red lava sand, as well as natal plum, African iris, royal palm, dwarf date palm, pampas grass,* lagerstroemia *(crape myrtle), bird-of-paradise and a bamboo hedge.*

Organized Abandon

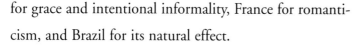

"My garden in São Paulo, Brazil, is an unframed picture with a solid architectural plan, with walls, flower beds and paths serving as structure. Although it was formally planned with clear visibility among its elements, it was informally planted using a great variety of specimens — azaleas and rhododendrons beneath leafy trees, clusters of bamboo, cypress and *Araucaria brasiliana* — creating separate garden spaces. Some are asymmetrical with no rigid pattern; others are symmetrical. Some are hidden, waiting to be discovered. I would call it a modern-style garden drawing from Italy for inspiration, England for grace and intentional informality, France for romanticism, and Brazil for its natural effect.

"To me, the garden is like food — it gives us energy and lightens our day. It also has colors which paint can't reproduce, and I like to fill ornamental pots throughout the garden and veranda with the seasonal gaiety of wild or hybrid flowers.

"We use our garden for dining and its nurturing spaces as a cozy refuge to relax and think while wandering. Because everything in it is natural, it is the most honest part in the home and lends to thought, word and action a certain freedom."

above *Ascending through this grove, one can count balls of* Juniperus sabina *as well as steps. The* Araucaria angustifolia *and* Tibouchina *trees are native to Brazil.*

Photography by Mauricio Simonetti

Neiva Rizzotto Landscape Designer

above *Complementing the home's earthy color are hydrangeas and nandinas placed in unregimented order along the pebble path.*

left *Daisies and agapanthus are among the seasonal flowers that bring a sense of change in areas close to the house throughout the year.*

Photography by Ricardo de Vicq de Cumptich

above *White jasmine climbs across a wooden arbor in an otherwise open field of* Juniperus sabina *pruned in the form of balls, with large native trees which are preferred by the designer because they grow old gracefully.*

above *Perfect after a walk through the woods, a fallen tree under a pergola provides exceptionally natural seating.*

Photography by Ricardo de Vicq de Cumptich

right *"I organized several garden areas asymmetrically with no rigid patterns, others symmetrically. The final result, when experienced as a whole, is a balance between landscape designed by man and nature itself." — Neiva Rizzotto*

A Challenging Site

"My garden in Southampton, New York, was used to solve a site problem — a narrow lot shaped like a flag that has a long shared driveway. By using the site's geometry and the easement's location to imply that the property is larger than it actually is, and by tying the garden's architecture with the style of the house, my partner Peter Shelton and I tried to synthesize all the disciplines so that the total result is greater than the sum of the parts.

"Working with landscape architect Nancy Haseley, horticulturist Richard Barrett and landscape installer Jody Shields, we divided the long front yard along the driveway into three square garden rooms separated by various hedges and gated fences. Thus, the driveway appears to be a foreign element cutting through an immense garden and severing the body of the house, whose separate parts are connected by a rose-covered pergola. The approach becomes a journey past three country garden rooms to what feels like a fourth: the more urban outdoor courtyard surrounded by the two fragments of the main house and the separate guest house.

"Extending the visual play, we graduated the height and size of the plantings and fences along the approach. Viewed from the house, the exaggerated depth provides a delightful illusion."

top *The three outdoor spaces of the flag lot as seen from the gate, divided by ewe hedges and bordered by coreopsis and roses. The gate is framed by potentilla.*

above *Viewed from the house, the street is masked from the garden by three outdoor rooms, foreshortened in this picture.*

Photography by Lee F. Mindel

Lee F. Mindel Architect

above *"The garden was used to solve a site problem. We tied the garden architecture and the interior together to synthesize all the disciplines so that the sum of the whole is, hopefully, greater than the individual parts."* — Lee F. Mindel

Portrait by William Abranowitz

left *At one corner of the pool, a canna lily is surrounded with plecostachy and sweet potato plants.*

top *The dining pavilion and swimming pool are masked by a fence, covered with* Petasites japonicus, *that defines the courtyard.*

above *An oculus by Andre Dubreuil, at the home's front doors, is in alignment with the front garden and allows visitors to relive their entry past the forecourt's three garden rooms.*

Lush Informality

Maarssen, Holland

"Situated on the river Vecht, our country house was built in 1725 on the foundations of a farm dating from as early as 1643. It is surrounded by a brick wall, a wonderful setting for a formal garden which indeed it was during its early life. However, the plot we found thirty years ago was a tangle of weeds. Planting a maythorn hedge around a quarter section of the space was the first step toward order. It encloses a salad patch and herb garden, with lettuces and thyme, lemon balm, arugula and currant bushes, reminiscent of the ancient farm. It provides, together with the lawn to its left, a setting for the temple, constructed of concrete and plywood.

"Seen from the house, the garden shows a more formal aspect. The undulating perennial borders with many old rambling roses are accentuated by clipped boxwood forms. All trees are fruit trees — the name of the house is 'The Orchard.' All garden work is done by me, as a welcome escape from my art history writing projects. I expect to work on this garden for a lifetime. I like it best when clients want me to design this kind of 'slow garden' for themselves."

above *A sharply shorn hawthorn hedge serves two goals. Seen from the house, it provides a formal setting for the temple. Seen from the temple, its undulating line reveals a rustic vegetable patch.*

Photography by Stephen Lewis

Loekie Schwartz Garden Historian/Designer

above *The landscape design moves the eye from one spot to the next. The carefully balanced forms and volumes provide a firm visual grip and induce a mood of peacefulness.*

left *A classical element was recently introduced by the construction of a temple. The materials are modern — concrete and plywood.*

above *A nineteenth-century tool shed, never restored, is a foil for the blue-leaved* Hosta sieboldiana *"Elegans," a quince and a honeysuckle.*

left *"I love the physical side of gardening and do everything myself. I mow the lawn, sieve the compost, plant, prune, and clip. Plans for a fountain, ideas for an article, a fitting idiom for a translation — all come easier pushing a wheelbarrow." — Loekie Schwartz*

below *Close to the house lies this small old-fashioned boxwood garden with shorn hedges and pyramids. The center is formed by a cube of variegated boxwood, surmounted by a ball. This form is borrowed from an emblem by the German poet Goethe. In his garden in Weimar he placed a stone ball on a cube to express the concept of "Quies" or calm. What more fitting image for a garden?*

Japanese Imprint

San Antonio, Texas

"The small space at the rear of my turn-of-the-century residence in San Antonio, Texas, yielded with great ease to a preference for a clean approach with Japanese leanings. While the projects I have designed with my late partner John Nichols have had widely varying guidelines, no one has requested such a simple exterior. This garden is a true reflection of a personal taste and also the desire for a low-maintenance space. Brick, decking, river rock and stone steps make up the hardscape. On the entire property, there is not one blade of grass to mow!

"The bamboo provides the natural screen needed for this narrow inner-city lot. A hearty Chinese plum, tree ferns and English ivy, as well as Durango river stone from Colorado and Leuders grey limestone from central Texas lend texture and color. For one sculptural note amid the sea of gravel, we added the Isamu Noguchi black granite fountain which was found at Stone Forest in Santa Fe.

"The garden and deck areas extend from the residence, studio and parking court as one continuous passage, making a calming transition zone as well as welcoming destination for meditation or conversation."

above *The garden and deck areas, which extend from the residence, studio and parking lot, are used constantly, their simplicity providing a calming transition zone.*

Photography by Peter Tata

Gari L. Sprott Interior Designer

above left *The bamboo, planted in 1975 by a previous owner, now creates a natural screen and the privacy intended for this thirty-eight-foot-wide inner-city lot in King William historic district.*

above *"After hectic work days, the soothing sound of water flowing over the black granite fountain designed by Isamu Noguchi provides the final note in making this environment ideal for meditation." — Gari L. Sprott*

left *The Durango River stone from Colorado was selected for its large size, which allows for easy leaf-blowing or raking without disturbing the rock.*

Cottage Garden

"My Washington Gardens in Fredericksburg, Virginia, is a stylized and finely appointed cottage garden on approximately one acre. The garden is a collection of many rare and unusual plants arranged for year-round enjoyment and situated according to culture as well as the interest of the foliage. Garden rooms, each with its own character, are connected with allées, oyster shell paths and other devices.

"Intensely planted with no ground showing, my garden's maintenance involves the prevention of 'thug-like' plants from overtaking meeker specimens. Many of the plants are arboretum experiments and thus unavailable for resale until we can prove them suitable.

"While the public is welcome from April until October and I even arrange catered tours and events here, my garden is truly a personal habitat for me and the birds. It is an extension of my feelings and my entire life, and I have incorporated many plants from relatives' and friends' gardens and see those people when I look at the plants. I have also used architectural details, such as the gingerbread arbor and fence, from my great aunt's house in Mississippi. She taught me how to love plants and through those details I think of her every day."

above *Variegated boxwood balls line this flagstone path and illuminate the walk at night. Cone flowers, summer phlox and tigerlilies populate the beds.*

Photography by Phillip Watson

Phillip Watson Garden Designer

left *The front garden is filled to the brim with colorful summer phlox and tigerlilies. The cottage walls are clad in variegated pyracantha "Harlequin" and Hollywood juniper. Copper window boxes contain verbena "Royal Ruby," a selection made from Phillip Watson's own seedling trials.*

above *A path of crushed oyster shell winds its way through towering boltonia "Snowbank" and sky blue salvia. The plumes of celosia "Flamingo Feather" punctuate the path while various low verbenas soften the edges.*

left *The black bottomed pool's reflective qualities double the view of the* Chamaecyparis *"Crippsii" hedge. The flamestich pattern allows glimpses into the adjacent garden.*

above *Golden yarrow and summer phlox color this poolside border while a white crape myrtle backlights the garden. Overhead, the golden fern-like foliage of gleditsia "Sunburst" lights the sky, while pots of silver artemisia and gold lysimachia brighten the front of the borders.*

right *"My garden began six years ago as a blank page — no trees, no walkways, and no foundation plantings."*
— Phillip Watson

left *The white gingerbread arbors stand out against an autumn sky and will continue to glow into the evening. Colorful cabbages and kale fill the garden, which is criss-crossed with white oyster shell paths. A Powis Castle artemisia standard flanks the bench.*

above *Impressive Thai string beans festoon the arbor and often reach lengths of two feet or more. However, they are usually harvested at about ten inches.*

left *A host of golden daffodils invites visitors to explore the winding oyster-shell path and to take a seat in the most fragrant part of the spring garden. The gazebo is an original design and can seat six for dinner.*

Mediterranean Style

Miami Beach, *Florida*

"The secluded garden within my Mediterranean revival villa in Miami Beach, Florida, is an extension of my passion for art and antiques, its classically proportioned spaces reflecting and surrounded by graciously formal Northern Italian architecture.

"My garden also reflects many of the places where I work — such as Windlesham Moor, Queen Elizabeth's early residence, and others in the Orient, the Middle East and Latin America. Each assignment exposes me to objects of art, antiquities and curiosities seldom seen at home. In my garden, I can place such treasures amid continual fragrance and gloriously colorful exotic flowers made possible by Florida's year-round tropical environment.

"I use my garden as a quiet escape from international travel. Also, its Tuscan fountain, antique consoles and chairs, hand-hewn chests and beams, terra-cotta tiled floors and pre-Columbian pottery and stone columns and arches, all dramatically illuminated at night, provide an elegant ambience for the parties my husband and I host. Either filled with friends and associates, or just myself alone, my garden is my refuge — with the sound of water from the fountain and the sea beyond playing music more tranquil, to me, than any other destination on earth."

above *The pool, on the home's ocean side, is shaped like a clover leaf with four semicircles that converge at four stone frogs, which spout thin lines of water into the center of the pool.*

Photography by Andrew Duany

Lynn Wilson Interior Designer

134

left *"When you have a setting of architecture and artifacts that make their own statement, the important thing is to subtly enhance the tranquility. In this private courtyard space, I have tried to accent but not overpower the atmosphere of harmony, beauty and peace."*
— *Lynn Wilson*

above *By night, halogen spotlights emphasize the fountain. Lynn Wilson's international art collection includes two Savonarola chairs and three pre-Columbian figures. Lagustrum trees surrounded by ivy and impatiens spill over the sides of 1920s Italian terracotta pots.*

EARTH SPIRITS

Lush Informality   Cultivating an Idea   Elevated Experiment

A Woodland Retreat   Balanced Integration

Creative Minimalism   Rustic Celebration   Jungle Paradise

A Garden Sequence   Period Vernacular

Freestyle Plantscape

Lush Informality

"My garden in Venice, California, is an informal yet comprehensive assemblage of plants. The home I renovated is on the coast and a 1920s mixture of Spanish, Santa Fe and Mediterranean styles. Within that context, I have established a lush tropical garden including cactuses and succulents, other drought-tolerant plants and an herb garden.

"This garden reflects the informality of my landscape designs for clients, yet here it is even more lush, reflecting my particular reverence for tropical plants. Being an architect as well as landscape designer, I always attempt to create a relationship between building and garden. This leads to paying particular attention to each site's climatic zone and the structure's orientation.

"Gardening is definitely part of my lifestyle. The herb garden allows me to grow plants such as tomatoes, basil and asparagus for cooking. The abundant exotic flowers are used in my arrangements. In addition, I enjoy the pleasure of designing, planting and even maintaining the garden.

"A garden is evolutionary, and here in Southern California one can live outdoors year-round, appreciating every stage of the garden as it exhibits an endless spectrum of colors, scents and textures. To me, this is a positive, uplifting force."

above *Palm fronds framing the smooth plaster finish of the home's portico, as well as the delicate violet of the princess flower, showy azalea and rhododendron, invite exploration of this delightfully multifaceted garden.*

Photography by Anthony Peres

Martin E. Bovill Architect/Landscape Architect

above *Tall, graceful king palms and giant bird-of-paradise plants act as anchors, and delicate fronds of a dicksonia tree fern contrast in size with the lushly layered tropical vegetation, providing an exotic, ever-changing landscape.*

overleaf *The kitchen opens onto an informal herb garden of thyme, oregano and basil mixed with artichokes, yarrow and globe thistle. Set within maroon and charcoal lava rock are the dramatically shaped Maui echeveria, fragrant plumeria and delicate snow cactus.*

left *"This garden reflects my goal — a dynamic and evolutionary palette of plant types and intimate scale that would create a sense of peace and contemplation."*
— *Martin E. Bovill*

Portrait by Barbara Heinzman

left *Drought-tolerant plants provide splashes of color and texture, including crassula, artemisia "Powis Castle" and bearded iris.*

opposite *Stately cactuses salute the two-story artist's studio beyond, with the distinguished escontria providing a focal point, while the heavily scented plumeria, distinctive barrel cactus, agave and varieties of hidden tillandsia (air plants) create a feast for the senses.*

Cultivating an Idea

"My husband and I had childhoods among orange groves. When we found Rancho Dulce, an orange ranch which produces more than fifty tons of Valencias each season, it seemed already fragrant with good memories. The ranch house, built of local stones from the Horn Canyon in the 1920s, contributed to the nostalgic feeling.

"I thought a great deal about the garden and the symbolic meaning of a garden located within such a cultivated grove surrounded by the young, rugged Topa Topa Mountains. I decided to celebrate the contrast between the cultivation of agriculture and the cultivation of the domicile garden by separating them with thick dry-mortar masonry walls. Further continuing the feeling of the layers of contrasting elements established by the surrounding mountains and groves, a series of interlocking rectangles includes a green rectangle of meadow grasses. Emphasizing the idea of 'cultivated house,' I invited other old roses to join an existing Cherokee rose in lacing the walls, grape arbor and front porch — a welcoming view from the entry's singular California pepper tree.

"This garden has been created by a process similar to how I work with clients, spending enough time to understand fully the existing situation before creating a structural diagram. The making of the garden becomes an act of inner cultivation and outer cultivation."

above *The grape arbor, centered between the groves and interior dwelling spaces, is truly the heart of the home.*

Photography by Pamela Burton

Pamela Burton Landscape Architect

above *Low mortared stone walls frame the newly planted green rectangle of buffalo and grama grasses, which will rarely need to be mowed.*

right *The front door is important because guests will use it only once, the first time they visit Rancho Dulce. The climbing "Cecil Brunner" rose blooms profusely each spring and holds the entry gracefully.*

below *Stone pilasters connected together with a stone bench separate the formal, first-time entry from the informal, everyday entry. Agave* pacifica, *blue oat grass, succulents and rockrose pedal down the path.*

above *"The ritual of reading a space while passing through it becomes an act essential to creating a garden."*
— Pamela Burton

opposite *A jacaranda throws its lavender blossoms onto a carpet of violets. The butter-cream-colored Cherokee rose with reverse-fishhook thorns is pruned often to make way for the rope swing.*

Elevated Experiment

"My garden in Santa Fe, New Mexico, is woven into the existing piñon and juniper tree cover which represents the area's primary natural vegetation. What makes the site unique is that, although close to the city's center, the vegetation is original and has never been disturbed. Therefore I have developed a modestly scaled landscape, consisting primarily of a narrow strip around the house that blends into the native vegetation. The style is informal and features a waterlily and goldfish pond.

"My garden is my experimental plot. I continually test out plants not considered hardy at Santa Fe's elevation of 7,000 feet. While I do not mind failure, clients need not tolerate it! Otherwise, my objectives apply both to my own and clients' gardens — plants that are attractive year-round, a mixture of evergreen and deciduous plants with long flowering periods, and the use of accent plants such as agaves and tall grasses.

"Much of my garden is visible from indoors, providing aesthetic and spiritual pleasure daily. I am in awe of the wonderful symmetry and soft gray blue of my agaves, and the pond attracts a wide variety of wildlife that I would otherwise not have an opportunity to view."

above *"To me, a garden represents the supreme expression of both personality and culture, and is always ultimately an experiment laden with surprises — some glorious and unexpected, some offensive and disappointing, which is a good analogy for life in general."*
— *Craig Campbell*

Photography by Craig Campbell

Craig Campbell Landscape Architect

above *The garden walk winds through a landscape punctuated by native perennials such as pine-leaf penstemon and non-native plants such as sunrose, ice plant and a hardy rosemary shrub.*

left *At home with the pond: waterlilies, narrow-leaf cattail, pickerel rush and iris.*

above *This agave,* Agave parryi, *is native to the southern part of New Mexico but has thrived in Santa Fe. The flowers, at the end of a thick stalk that reaches 18 feet in height, attract both hummingbirds and orioles.*

right *The stream, with recirculated pond water, was built by Craig Campbell from rounded rocks collected from the local arroyo. Dianthus borders both sides of the stream, which is visible from the home's dining room and attracts a wide variety of birds otherwise rarely seen in the city.*

A Woodland Retreat

"My garden in Atlanta is a recreation of my childhood memories, my mother's garden, my travels and my desire for a tropical environment. My business is product development and the marketing of home and garden furnishings. However, my own garden is simply and completely a personal reflection.

"Although the pool, stone walls and walkways were contracted, my wife Suzy and I do ninety-five percent of the gardening. We always are adding and subtracting, making sure that when you swim in the pool you see nothing but plants for a totally remote feeling, encouraging trees to frame, roses and wisteria to climb over guest house and fences, and soft mosses and ferns to softly cover our woodland floor. We also like working with fragrance.

"How do you have such a garden without it becoming part of your lifestyle? We use the garden for exercise, entertainment and meditation — as a source of tranquility. I regularly tell my neighbors to get busy doing something in their yards. There is an absolute sense of renewal. The religious myths of mankind are clarified through the experience of spring, summer, fall, winter and then the rebirth of spring."

above *The house is covered with Boston ivy, which turns a vibrant red in the fall. On the wall in the foreground is a red trumpet vine, and to its right are fig trees and a Concord grape vine that has borne fruit for twenty years.*

Photography by David Schilling

Robert Currey Designer

above *The garden continues on the deck, with an herb garden on the teak table, a potted banana tree and autumn clematis on the railing. The left side of the pool and garden is shaded by a magnificent oak tree in the neighbor's yard.*

left *"Our garden has a mesmerizing quality, is a balm for the spirit, and offers a tranquility to the eye. It's hard to leave."*
— Robert Currey

left *The walkway from the front into the backyard garden consists of a grassy path with steps of Tennessee fieldstone and lined with boxwood and pots of holly.*

Balanced Integration

East Hampton, *New York*

"Its potential garden is the reason I started to build this home in East Hampton, New York, in 1968. Ever since, it has continued to evolve — around additions of pool, gazebo, studio — as I, my wife Catherine and landscape architect Edmund Hollander have endeavored to blend living needs with the desire to keep the feeling natural.

"In trying to achieve the right balance of hardscape with naturescape, I have become increasingly intrigued by the proportion of one to the other, an ever-changing aspect of landscape design. Trees and plants live, grow and die and they look different throughout the seasons. Not only do they need pruning and transplanting, their sizes change, thus making that all-important aspect of proportion a flexible element. Yet ideally, the garden should look good in relationship to the built structures at all times, from youth to maturity and from spring to winter. It is important to predict these changes and plan for them.

"Here the prominent goal has been to emphasize the property's stand of white pines — cutting out and pruning unwanted species so that these treasures maintain their assertiveness. Yet it is also important to cultivate new growth for a sense of shelter on a human scale."

above *The west side of the house overlooks an outdoor room with a small pool where a lavender daylily blooms. The enclosure is paved in bluestone squares, patterned to enclose planting which includes ornamental flowering shrubs, perennials and a Kousa dogwood.*

Photography by Judith Watts

reprinted by permission of *House Beautiful*, copyright © October 1992. The Hearst Corporation. All rights reserved.

Alfredo De Vido Architect

above *"The juxtaposition of the built structure with the landscape can, and therefore should, enhance each other. To me, the Japanese idea of poising a building within nature is the most inspired perspective."* — *Alfredo De Vido*

right *Beyond the silhouette of a halesia tree, Caesar's Brother iris, cinnamon ferns and astilbe stand before the pool filled with hardy waterlilies. Further surrounding the pool, from left, are mountain laurel, a Franklinia tree, more cinnamon ferns and astilbe, a leucothoe shrub, inkberry, magnolia, dogwood, miniature iris and assorted daylilies.*

Creative Minimalism

"My garden in Santa Barbara, California, is merely six feet by forty feet — a narrow slot between my condominium and the neighbor's fence that I have turned into a green tunnel with all the amenities. They include deck and lounge chair, table for four, a parasol and a tree wisteria in a pot that rolls on wheels to give shade wherever I want. In fact, all the potted plants on my deck are on wheels so I can hose and sweep under them and prevent the deck from deteriorating. At any rate, to my great surprise, I have created exactly what I do for others, following all the same processes, the same sequence, the same order.

"First I altered the condo to better relate to the garden. Then came circulation — deck, steps and stepping-stones. Then came the genteel arrangement of my utility area and anaerobic composters. Finally, utilization of the neighbor's fence into a vertical herbal/vegetable garden. There is still room for birdbath, pond with its bog-simulating iris and such old roses, favorite shrubs, miniature trees (including my bonsai crab apple!) and other potted friends that have been with me for twenty years.

"Wherever I've lived, I have always had an 'enormous' garden."

above *To enlarge the rooms and enable them to open onto the garden, the window openings were changed into French doors. The addition of some raised decking, level with the floors, also enlarges the rooms and invites one directly outside.*

opposite *While conventional wood steps are used elsewhere, these steps were created from found stone pieces — including old curbs and hitching posts. The addition of a greenhouse window takes the kitchen right into the garden.*

Photography by Anthony Peres

Isabelle Greene Landscape Architect

above *"In front of my favorite bench sit two old rotting stumps that, in their prime, served as little mini-tables, but they soon passed into severe decline so I planted wild white aster around them. Soon aster and stumps had joined together like longtime friends."*
— Isabelle Greene

left *Deciding that she could not bear to have hard surface meet hard surface without plants in between, Greene provided small planting holes in the deck, fitted out with copper liners. Flourishing in these 12 x 18 x 18 inch soil pockets are espaliered apple trees (with 40-apple crops!) as well as fragrant stephanotis.*

opposite *The birdbath is fed by quarter-inch copper pipe with two valves regulating the water so it drips every seventh second. This keeps the birdbath brimming and dropping occasionally into the space below — a small lily pond surrounded by bog- and water-loving iris and reeds.*

Rustic Celebration

"My love affair with this home started decades ago, when landscape specialist Emmet Wemple took me to visit architect Allen Siple's creation in Los Angeles's Mandeville Canyon. It was an extraordinary experience — absorbing the home's formidable masonry and weathered wood surrounded by huge sycamores — every stone, every wooden beam installed by Siple himself. Years later, after Siple had died and I purchased the property, I felt I had come home. Despite all the futuristic complexes I am asked to create, my work is based on linking humanity and nature — and this was Siple's vision. Both are celebrations of life.

"I use the garden for meditation, but Janice actually gardens. In terms of plant material, we are in constant flux, changing by season and by mood, following our preference for a visually ungroomed look as well as aromatic plants, such as jasmine, thyme and rosemary. These previously nonexistent gardens and lawns we developed over time with landscape architect Marian Cobb, keeping in mind first our children's needs and then aesthetics. We have made few architectural changes, save for the carved Indonesian columns and the outdoor fireplace — but we're still waiting for it to acquire the appropriate patina to go with what Siple wrought."

above *Mature sycamores stand as eternal beacons to Jon Jerde's memories of his first visit, with the late, renowned landscape architect Emmet Wemple, to Allen Siple's house.*

Photography by Tim Street-Porter

Jon A. Jerde Architect

Janice Ambry Jerde Architect

right *The home's formidable presence of stone masonry, alleviated by only a few small windows, is softened by a frame of ivy and impatiens.*

Photography by Ralph Yanagawa

above *"I garden, while Jon more often uses the outdoor spaces to read and create. But always, the whole family enjoys its specialness."*
— Janice and Jon A. Jerde with their son Oliver, and Hattie.

Photography by Tim Street-Porter

left *Designed by the Jerdes of stone from the surrounding canyon, this barbecue area is another way in which the architects have furthered their indoor/outdoor lifestyle.*

Photography by Tim Street-Porter

Jungle Paradise

"Given the fact that my residence faces a tropical jungle, I designed my garden to continue the jungle's life-enhancing exuberance. Even in other projects in which the landscape design is more governed by the architecture, I lean toward a natural rather than a very planned atmosphere. Besides, due to Panama's tropical climate, we have access to a wide variety of exotic foliage plants that grow almost instantly and enhance the environment tremendously.

"To my wife Sandra and me, the garden is an indispensable complement to our house. It surrounds and completely embraces our home and can be felt from every room. Its force has absorbed us. Since we experience the jungle's atmosphere without excluding its other inhabitants, such as iguanas, toucans, monkeys, squirrels and snakes, our garden is alive. It moves, sings and interacts with our lifestyle. Also, as our house opens onto the garden, the garden is used daily, with all gatherings flowing between inner and outer areas.

"A garden is not only visually beautiful. The sound of the breeze rushing through the bamboo leaves, the sun's turning the trees into a play of light, the capacity of plants to produce oxygen ... all are a tremendous source of power."

above *A concrete frog, like most of the ornaments in this garden, was recovered from one of many buildings dating from Panama's colonial period.*

opposite *Gathered around an ornamental torch are Dracaena marginata, Amomum cardamon "ginger," "silver evergreen" Aglaonema, Hemigraphis colorata "red ivy," tall feather fern, Calathea picturata vandenheckie, zebra plant and aluminum plants.*

Photography by Enoch Castillero C.

Ignacio Mallol III Architect

162

left *"Gardens are not only beautiful for their color and their exuberance. Their beauty and power lie in the ways they create sound and light effects and provide oxygen to enhance our lives." — Ignacio Mallol III*

above *In this part of the garden, an adult Chinese banyan and a potted jungle geranium join a colony of yellow bamboo.*

right *From every vantage point, the living room provides views of the garden through the architecture's generous use of floor-to-ceiling windows.*

opposite *In the foreground, a bamboo lane leads into the garden's jungle section, while a primitive architectural form exudes the environment's native spirit.*

A Garden Sequence

"One block from the Malibu beach, my garden is one-half acre of four ponds surrounded by a variety of areas where I try out new and unusual species. I am interested particularly in those that are clay-soil-tolerant and drought-resistant, and even the cutting garden is drip-irrigated.

"Yet the garden also is ideal for other pursuits. The property is divided throughout by partitions. 'Walls' of pampas grass, umbrella palms and massive clumps of asparagus fern create sequestered nooks that are protected from the prevailing afternoon winds. One area, near the propagation pond, is where I work on my laptop computer, the trickling stream serving as my natural music system. An easy chair is positioned by a tub fountain and is perfectly shaded for solitary reading. The graveled conversation patio is secluded by potted plants and papyrus, seemingly far from the house. The table and chairs, used for client meetings and entertaining, are surrounded by tub gardens filled with bog plants and waterlilies. Behind the garage, a hot tub provides just the place to enjoy the fragrance of wisteria in the spring, datura in the summer, and night-blooming jasmine in the fall."

above *The reading chair is protected from wind and afternoon sun by a yellow champaca, a magnolia and papyrus. The pond, teeming with tropical nymphae and fiber optics grass, cools the air as well as refreshens the spirit.*

Photography by Andy Rice

Carolyn Mitchell Landscape Designer

left *"I favor the use of under-utilized trees and plants for basic form and structure, while my goal always is to achieve hydrozoning and landscape sustainability."* — *Carolyn Mitchell*

above *Far from the house, the secluded conversation patio is surrounded by the property's ubiquitous water features — tub gardens filled with bog plants and small, hardy waterlilies.*

Period Vernacular

"My garden in Pasadena is much a local garden, blessed with wonderful indigenous elements. The boulders came from the nearby Arroyo Seco and were, before their current exalted state, the stepchildren of an earlier effort at gardening. That was before life began, I think. The three magnificent California live oaks, which probably predate my earliest California ancestors, create an ever-changing lacework of light as the sun passes on its daily trek through the sky. Because I had designed my office to nest near the heart of one of these treasured trees, I was keenly aware of the theater of light they create. It became an important element in the garden I planned.

"My main house is a 1907 Craftsman and my guest house, an even more venerable Victorian farmhouse. Much of my work has been centered around Pasadena's older housing stock, conditioning me to think in a slightly modernized (mechanically enhanced) period vernacular. The studio's newly redesigned deck, handrail and building details reflect this internalized experience of Pasadena's history. The garden, of course, responded.

"Stolen moments at the stream never cease to please my mind and body, reminding me of joyful hours spent hiking in the local mountains or fly-fishing on grander waters."

above *California live oaks coalesce with the studio, providing bones for this landscape that includes salvaged brick and planters containing oakleaf hydrangea, liriope, island alum root and clivia. Decomposed granite surrounding the oaks offers protection from water and possible root fungus.*

opposite *Boulders handselected at the quarry for an earlier landscape have been recycled into a free-stone stream planted with hosta, liriope, island alum root, bergenia, sedge, Pacific Coast iris and chenille plant.*

Joan Moseley Designer/Contractor

Photography by Anthony Peres

above *"In my 'micro' marsh at the source of the stream, we built a rock seat which feels as if it responds perfectly to my body's natural posture. Sitting there, I can lose myself in the light, the texture and the healing sounds of this place. Bliss. Local, available, ever-ready. Sweet and sure. Heaven."*
— *Joan Moseley*

left *Indigenous boulders and river-washed gravel edge the pond, while a pathway of shredded redwood bark leads through the streambed. Chenille plant, sedges and bergenia abound in a small grove of Japanese maples and surrounds coffeeberry scrubs. The garden furniture is vintage American Hickory.*

Photography by Anthony Peres

left *Detailing inspired by architects Charles Sumner Greene and Henry Mather Greene for the clear-heart redwood deck combines with reproduction Craftsman lighting to create a passage between the main house/studio and the guest house. Low plantings are of island alum root, oakleaf hydrangea, liriope, bergenia, and ferns.*

left *This small seating area, surrounded by Japanese maples and set against the backdrop of California live oaks, oversees sword ferns in the distance, the lawn of St. Augustine, and the foreground planted with Pacific Coast iris, chenille plants, bergenia and sedge.*

Photography by Anthony Peres

right *The massive arm of a California live oak echoes the studio's clerestory windows. Boxed Japanese maple and staghorn ferns are visible beneath the redwood deck. Liriope mass in a planter running the length of the patio, made of brick chosen to complement the clinker brick details of the main house.*

above *Light is probably the most important element in this garden. The various materials, whether of the landscape or of the structure, were chosen to reflect, filter and receive light as part of their roles in this drama.*

Freestyle Plantscape

"Our garden in Big Sur, California, is on an oak ridge. The wooded east side is arranged in rather rectilinear terraces of native stone; the west side terraces are more freeform and planted with palms, citrus, loquat, and native flowering shrubs.

"While Sherna's gardens for clients are more garden-like, more manicured, more intensely planted with color, our own garden, evolved over twenty-five years, reflects a desire to stay close to the natural landscape we found here. Order was introduced simply with hedges and with stone walls and crushed rock paving. The paving makes it easy to alter planting if we choose and also reduces runoff during our heavy winter rains. Except for the palms, the plants are generally drought resistant.

"We find the garden is a very tolerant place. It prospers whether it's neglected or subjected to excess zeal. Unlike architecture or interior decors, gardens grow, revealing to us the wonderful spontaneity of life itself, beyond human contrivance."

above *The view beyond Kipp Stewart's studio is composed of a loquat, a bank of fatsia with a bamboo hedge, small Mediterranean palms and a table and chair designed by the architect for Bradford Stewart & Company.*

Photography by Kipp Stewart

Kipp Stewart Architect
Sherna Stewart Landscape Designer

above *The deck outside the kitchen, which faces south to the Big Sur coastline and opens to a forty-mile view of bays and headlands, is turned into an outdoor room by the overhead trellis. The teak chaise was designed by Kipp Stewart for the Summit Furniture Company.*

opposite *Beyond the deck teeming with potted begonias and overseen by California oaks, a distant hedge of* Pittosporum undulatum *defines a large square garden space.*

right *"While this garden goes on changing and developing over the years, there are many hours in which we simply sit and enjoy."*
— Kipp and Sherna Stewart

above *Looking past the bedroom and living room toward the Pacific Ocean and miles of Big Sur coastline.*

left *A lively apricot-colored bougainvillea graces the west wall of the house, creating a friendly contrast to the pine shutters and weathered redwood exterior.*

DIRECTORY

ARCHITECTS, DESIGNERS & LANDSCAPE ARCHITECTS

Robert Bellamy
Robert Bellamy Design
1918 North Prairie
Dallas, Texas 75204
Tel: (214) 826-4612
Fax: (214) 823-7274

Dale Booher and Lisa Stamm
The Homestead Garden and
    Design Collaborative
Box 90, Shelter Island Heights,
    New York 11965
Tel: (516) 749-2189
Fax: (516) 749-3417

Martin E. Bovill, AIA
Martin Bovill & Associates
821 Crestmoore Place
Venice, California 90291
Tel/Fax: (310) 827-2185

Karen Dominguez Brann
Foxglove Design
P.O. Box 582
Malibu, California 90265
Tel: (818) 880-9216

Erika Brunson
Erika Brunson Design Associates
903 Westbourne Drive
Los Angeles, California 90069
Tel: (310) 652-1970
Fax: (310) 652-2381

Pamela Burton, ASLA
Pamela Burton & Co.
2324 Michigan Avenue
Santa Monica, California 90404
Tel: (310) 828-6373
Fax: (310) 828-8054

Craig Campbell, FASLA
Design Workshop, Inc.
660 17th Street, Suite 325
Denver, Colorado 80202
Tel: (303) 623-5186
Fax: (303) 623-2260

Jack Chandler, ASLA
Jack Chandler & Associates
P.O. Box 2180
Yountville, California 94599
Tel: (707) 944-8352
Fax: (707) 944-0651

Robert Currey
Currey & Company, Inc.
200 Ottley Drive, N.E.
Atlanta, Georgia 30324
Tel: (404) 885-1444
Fax: (404) 885-1199

Hugh Dargan, ASLA
Mary Palmer Dargan, ASLA
Hugh Dargan Associates, Inc.
515 East Paces Ferry Road
Atlanta, Georgia 30305
Tel: (404) 231-3889
Fax: (404) 231-5494

Alfredo De Vido, FAIA
Alfredo De Vido Associates
1044 Madison Avenue
New York, New York 10021
Tel: (212) 517-6100
Fax: (212) 517-6103

Ron Goldman, FAIA
Goldman Firth Boccato
24955 Pacific Coast Highway
Malibu, California 90265
Tel: (310) 456-1831
Fax: (310) 456-7690

Michael Graves, FAIA
Michael Graves, Architect
341 Nassau Street
Princeton, New Jersey 08540
Tel: (609) 924-6409
Fax: (609) 924-1795

Isabelle Greene, ASLA
Isabelle Greene & Associates
2613 De La Vina Street
Santa Barbara, California 93105
Tel: (805) 569-4045
Fax: (805) 569-2270

Ron Hefler
    Ron Hefler
    David Graham
465 South Sweetzer Avenue
Los Angeles, California 90048
Tel: (213) 651-1231
Fax: (213) 735-2502

**Hendrix/Allardyce, A Design
    Corporation**
Thomas Allardyce
Illya Hendrix
335 North La Cienega Boulevard
Los Angeles, California 90048
Tel: (213) 654-2222
Fax: (310) 657-6130

**Douglas Pierce Hiatt, ASID,
    IFDA, BIID**
Hiatt Enterprises International, Inc.
9454 Wilshire Boulevard, Suite 650
Beverly Hills, California 90212
Tel: (310) 275-5389
Fax: (310) 275-6890

Allison A. Holland, ASID
Creative Decorating
168 Poloke Place
Honolulu, Hawaii 96822
Tel: (808) 955-1465
Fax: (808) 943-8450

**Lucia Howard and David
    Weingarten**
Ace Architects
The Leviathan
330 Second Street, No. 1
Oakland, California 94607
Tel: (510) 452-0775
Fax: (510) 452-1175

Takekuni Ikeda, Ph.D.
Nihon Sekkei, Inc.
Shijuku Mitsui Building, 43rd Floor
2-1-1 Nishi Shinjuku
Shinjuku-ku, Tokyo 163-04
Japan
Tel: 81 3 5325 8686
Fax: 81 3 3344 0730

Janice Ambry Jerde, AIA
Ambry & Associates
913 Ocean Front Walk
Venice, California 90291
Tel: (310) 399-2404
Fax: (310) 392-7102

Jon A. Jerde, FAIA
The Jerde Partnership
    International, Inc.
913 Ocean Front Walk
Venice, California 90291
Tel: (310) 399-1987
Fax: (310) 392-1316

Lory Johansson
Ergo Design Works, Inc.
8112 1/2 West Third Street, Suite D
Los Angeles, California 90048
Tel: (213) 658-8901
Fax: (213) 658-8903

Carol Soucek King, Ph.D.
Carol Soucek King Enterprises
60 El Circulo Drive
Pasadena, California 91105
Tel: (818) 449-1238
Fax: (818) 449-2004

**Linda Merrifield Kinninger,
    ASID, IIDA, AIA Affiliate**
The Designing Women
800 Foothill Boulevard
La Canada Flintridge,
    California 91011
Tel: (818) 790-7803
Fax: (818) 790-7519

Scott Larimer
Four Seasons Garden Center
312 North Logan Street
Mattoon, Illinois 61938
Tel: (217) 235-1197
Fax: (217) 235-4836

Michael La Rocca
Michael R. La Rocca, Ltd.
150 East 58th Street, #3510
New York, New York 10155
Tel: (212) 755-5558
Fax: (212) 838-3034

Jack Lenor Larsen
Jack Lenor Larsen
233 Spring Street
New York, New York 10003
Tel: (212) 462-1300
Fax: (212) 462-1313

Mia Lehrer
Mia Lehrer Landscape Architecture
2227 Talmadge Street
Los Angeles, California 90027-2917
Tel: (213) 664-3419
Fax: (213) 664-3566

Ignacio Mallol III
Mallol & Mallol Arquitectos
6-0040 Estafeta El Dorado
Panama City
Republic of Panama
Tel: (507) 264-4657/223-0436
Fax: (507) 223-0131

Lee F. Mindel, AIA
Shelton, Mindel & Associates
216 West 18th Street
New York, New York 10011
Tel: (212) 243-3939
Fax: (212) 727-7310

Carolyn Mitchell
Carolyn Mitchell Landscape Design
6749 Wildlife Road
Malibu, California 90265
Tel: (310) 457-6133

Donald Monger
The Landmark Group
Oxley House, Level 2
25 Donkin Street
South Brisbane
Australia 4101
Tel: (61 7) 3846 7300
Fax: (61 7) 3846 7522

Juan Montoya
Juan Montoya Design Corporation
80 Eighth Avenue, 16th Floor
New York, New York 10011
Tel: (212) 242-3622
Fax: (212) 242-3743

Joan Moseley
Joan Moseley Design
649 La Loma Road
Pasadena, California 91105
Tel: (818) 799-1578
Fax: (818) 799-6967

James W. P. Olson, FAIA
Olson Sundberg, Architects
108 First Avenue, South
Seattle, Washington 98104
Tel: (206) 624-5670
Fax: (206) 624-3730

Rick Orr, AIFD
Rick Orr Florist
122 North Walnut Street
Champaign, Illinois 61820
Tel: (217) 351-9299

Carlos Pascal, IIDA,
Gerard Pascal, IIDA
Pascal Arquitectos
Atlaltunco 99, Tecamachalco
Estado de Mexico
C.P. 53950
Mexico
Tel: (525) 294 2371
Fax: (525) 294 8513

Neiva Rizzotto
Rua Sofia, 75 Jardim Europa
01447-030 São Paulo
Brazil
Tel: (55) 11 852-1977
Fax: (55) 11 282-1385

Loekie Schwartz
De Boomgaard
Herengracht 22
3601 Am Maarssen
Holland
Tel: 31 3 465 62778
Fax: 31 3 465 70574

Martha Schwartz
Martha Schwartz, Inc.
167 Pemberton Street
Cambridge, Massachusetts 02140
Tel: (617) 661-8141
Fax: (617) 661-8707

Bill and Erika Shank
Shank Design Associates, Inc.
83 Wooster Street, #4
New York, New York 10012-4376
Tel: (212) 925-4070
Fax: (212) 966-0527

Mabel Shults
Mabel Shults & Associates
217 State Street, #200
Santa Barbara, California 93110
Tel: (805) 965-8699
Fax: (805) 965-0897

Gari L. Sprott
Sprott-Nichols Design
335 Madison
San Antonio, Texas 78204
Tel: (210) 224-1885
Fax: (210) 224-1887

Kipp and Sherna Stewart
Post Office Drawer 6145
Carmel, California 93921
Tel: (408) 624-8969

David Walker
David Walker, Inc.
19 Commerce Street
New York, New York 10014
Tel: (212) 337-0085
Fax: (212) 337-0774

Phillip Watson
Washington Gardens
1008 Clearview Avenue
Fredericksburg, Virginia 22405
Tel: (540) 373-1972
Fax: (540) 373-6345

Lynn Wilson, ASID
Lynn Wilson Associates
   International
116 Alhambra Circle
Coral Gables, Florida 33134
Tel: (305) 442-4041
Fax: (305) 443-4276

James J. Yoch
The Garden Studio
623 Okmulgee
Norman, Oklahoma 73071
Tel: (405) 321-6042
Fax: (405) 321-6063

PHOTOGRAPHERS

William Abranowitz
Art & Commerce
755 Washington Street
New York, New York 10014
Tel: (212) 206-0737
Fax: (212) 463-7267

Jerome Adamstein
Phto/Dzn
153 South Robertson Boulevard
Los Angeles, California 90048
Tel: (310) 288-3879
Fax: (310) 288-3884

Glen Allison
Tel: (310) 842-4962
Fax (U.S.):
(800) 596-9421
Fax (outside U.S.):
(510) 927-2785

Jaime Ardiles-Arce
730 Fifth Avenue
New York, New York 10010
Tel: (212) 686-4220

Tom Bonner
Tom Bonner Photography
1201 Abbot Kinney Boulevard
Venice, California 90291
Tel: (310) 396-7125
Fax: (310) 396-4792

Bob Bronson
Bronson Photography
2060 Montrose Avenue
Montrose, California 91020
Tel: (818) 249-5864
Fax: (818) 249-2260

Marek Bulaj
Michael Graves, Architect
341 Nassau Street
Princeton, New Jersey 08540
Tel: (609) 924-6409
Fax: (609) 924-1795

Enoch Castillero C.
Industria Fotografica Lito Arte S.A.
Enoch Foto Estudio
Apartado 1135, Zona 9A,
Panama City
Republic of Panama
Tel: (507) 263-7920/264-8225
Fax: (507) 269-2246

Jared Chandler
Jack Chandler & Associates
P.O. Box 2180
Yountville, California 94599
Tel: (707) 944-8352
Fax: (707) 944-0651

Ricardo de Vicq de Cumptich
Rua Pedro Teixeira, 91
São Paulo
Brazil
Tel: (55) 11 530-5549
Fax: (55) 11 530-5282

Andrew Duany
Photography by Andrew
1007 S.W. 112th Terrace
Pembroke Pines, Florida 33025
Tel: (305) 430-4651
Fax: (305) 430-4651

Eitan Feinholz
Pascal Arquitectos
Atlaltunco 99, Tecamachalco
Estado de Mexico
C.P. 53970
Mexico
Tel: (525) 294 2371
Fax: (525) 294 8513

Mark Fiennes
29 Therapia Road
London SE 22 OSF
United Kingdom
Tel/Fax: (081) 299-0763

Mick Hales
Greenworld Pictures, Inc.
North Richardsville Road, RD#2
Carmel, New York 10512
Tel/Fax: (914) 228-0106

Barbara Heinzman
1518 South Crest Drive
Los Angeles, California 90035
Tel: (310) 551-0868

Douglas Hill
2324 Moreno Drive
Los Angeles, California 90039
Tel: (213) 660-0681

Michael Jensen
655 N.W. 76th Street
Seattle, Washington 98117
Tel: (206) 789-7963

Kenneth Johansson
Tel: (310) 828-0619

Elliott Kaufman
Elliott Kaufman Photography
255 West 90th Street
New York, New York 10024
Tel: (212) 496-0860
Fax: (212) 496-9104

Barry Lewis
Barry Lewis Photography, Inc.
2401 South Ervay Street, #306
Dallas, Texas 75215
Tel: (214) 421-5665
Fax: (214) 421-2007

Stephen Lewis
900 Union Street
Brooklyn, New York 11215
Tel: (718) 399-0494
Fax: (718) 399-0494

David Livingston
1036 Erica Road
Mill Valley, California 94941
Tel: (415) 383-0898
Fax: (415) 383-0897

Andrew McKinney
McKinney Photography
180 1/2 10th Avenue
San Francisco, California 94118
Tel: (415) 752-4070
Fax: (415) 752-0152

Mary E. Nichols
132 South Beachwood Drive
Los Angeles, California 90004
Tel: (213) 935-3080
Fax: (213) 935-9788

Tomio Ohashi
Ikeda Institute
29th Floor, Shinjuku I-Land Tower
6-5-1 Nishi-Shinjuku
Shinjuku-ku, Tokyo 163-13
Japan
Tel: (81) 3 5325 8686
Fax: (81) 3 5325 8688

Edy Owen
Photo Support Services
391 East Delamore Drive
Henderson, Nevada 89015
Tel/Fax: (702) 564-2274

Anthony Peres
Anthony Peres Photographer
645 Oxford Avenue
Venice, California 90291
Tel/Fax: (310) 821-1984

Douglas Piburn
335 North La Cienega Boulevard
Los Angeles, California 90048
Tel: (213) 654-2222
Fax: (310) 657-6130

Undine Prohl
1930 Ocean Avenue, #302
Santa Monica, California 90405
Tel/Fax: (310) 399-5031

Marvin Rand
Marvin Rand Photography
1310 Abbot Kinney Boulevard
Venice, California 90291
Tel: (310) 396-3441
Fax: (320) 396-2366

Andy Rice
Andy Rice Photography
7226 Rue de Roark
La Jolla, California 92037
Tel: (619) 459-8484

Augie Salbosa
Augie Salbosa Photography
1317 Kalakaua Avenue
Honolulu, Hawaii 96826
Tel: (808) 949-8598
Fax: (808) 955-6733

Durston Saylor
H. Durston Saylor, Inc.
175 Fifth Avenue
New York, New York 10010
Tel: (212) 228-2468
Fax: (201) 783-5573

David Schilling
Schilling Photography
1816 E Briarwood Industrial Court
Atlanta, Georgia 30329
Tel: (404) 636-1399
Fax: (404) 633-1572

Erika R. Shank
83 Wooster Street
New York, New York 10012
Tel: (212) 925-4070
Fax: (212) 925-0527

Shinkenchiku-sha Co. Ltd.
c/o Ikeda Institute
29th Floor, Shinjuku I-Land Tower
6-5-1 Nishi-Shinjuku
Shinjuku-ku, Tokyo 163-13
Japan
Tel: (81) 3 5325 8686
Fax: (81) 3 5325 8688

Mauricio Simonetti
Rua Francisco Cruz, 428 - casa 4
São Paulo
Brazil
Tel: (55) 11 575 2917

Tim Street-Porter
2074 Watsonia Terrace
Los Angeles, California 90068
Tel: (213) 874-4278
Fax: (213) 876-8795

Peter Tata
Peter Tata Photography
3306 Bridle Path
Austin, Texas 78703
Tel: (512) 320-0688
Fax: (512) 320-0112

Jill Van Hoogenstyn
Jill Van Hoogenstyn Photography
1928 North Verdugo Road
Glendale, California 91208
Tel: (818) 548-4461

Jay Venezia
1373 Edgecliffe Drive
Los Angeles, California 90027
Tel: (213) 665-7382

Peter Vitale
P.O. Box 10126
Santa Fe, New Mexico 87504
Tel: (505) 988-2558
Fax: (505) 982-6412

Alan Ward
P.O. Box 344
Newtown Branch
Boston, Massachusetts 02258
Tel: (617) 926-3300
Fax: (617) 924-2748

Judith Watts
House Beautiful
1700 Broadway
New York, New York 10019
Tel: (212) 903-5084
Fax: (212) 765-8292

Dave Weaver, Jr.
401 1/2 East Michigan Avenue
Urbana, Illinois 61801
Tel: (217) 328-7320

Alan Weintraub
Alan Weintraub Photography
1832 A Mason Street
San Francisco, California 94133
Tel: (415) 553-8191
Fax: (415) 553-8192

Charles S. White
Charles White Photography
154 North Mansfield Avenue
Los Angeles, California 90036
Tel: (213) 937-3117
Fax: (213) 937-1808

Ralph Yanagawa
The Jerde Partnership, Inc.
913 Ocean Front Walk
Venice, California 90291
Tel: (310) 399-1987
Fax: (310) 392-1316

INDEX

ACKNOWLEDGMENTS

It has been a privilege and a pleasure to develop the idea for this book with PBC International, Inc. *Empowered Gardens* could not have been realized without the foresight of Publisher Mark Serchuck regarding today's tremendous interest in gardening. He has understood that this vigorous greening trend, amid an increasingly technological world that often seems opposed to nature, is based on people's psychological and spiritual as well as physical needs to maintain a connection to Earth's beauty and nurturing power.

Managing Editor Susan Kapsis has worked with me daily on this thought so that it might be developed correctly in our presentation of the personal gardens of architects, designers and landscape specialists. Her taste and her professionalism raise books in her charge to a higher level and I am most grateful to have had her support once again with this volume.

PBC's Technical Director Richard Liu has lent his expert analysis of all photographic material. Designer Garrett Schuh has interpreted the subject with unusual sensitivity, illuminating the pages of this book with his creativity and deep sensibility. Nicholas Sica, Daniela Graziose, Annette Dippolito and Caroline Beckenhaupt have supported the process constantly with their attention to detail. And once again I am indebted to my longtime associate Angeline Vogl for her careful reading of the manuscript.

Among others who have been especially helpful with this volume are Nihon Sekkei's Akira Hashimoto and landscape architects Chirstopher Cos and the late Emmet Wemple. I also am grateful to the many architects, designers, landscape specialists and photographers whose work fills the pages of this book as well as to Michael Graves for graciously contributing the foreword.